THE OFFICIAL

Arsenal

FANS' GUIDE

THIS IS A CARLTON BOOK

This edition published in 1997

10 9 8 7 6 5 4 3 2 1

A CIP catalogue record for this book is available from the British Library

ISBN 1 85868 410 2

Project Editor: Martin Corteel
Project art direction: Paul Messam
Production: Garry Lewis and Sarah Schuman
Picture research: Sarah Moule
Designed by Adam Wright

Author's acknowledgements
First to Aidan, my son, who returned home from university just in time
to render enormous assistance in both the research and writing.
Secondly to Lynn, my wife, for battling her way through the statistical
and historical research. Beyond them, to Martin Corteel and the editorial
team at Carlton Books, notably Gavin Hamilton, Phil Wisdom and
David Ballheimer, for turning around so much in so short a time.

Printed in Italy

THE OFFICIAL

Arsenal

FANS' GUIDE

THE STORY OF
THE PREMIER LEAGUE YEARS

KEIR RADNEDGE

CARLTON

Contents

Tony Adams has led Arsenal back to success

The team celebrates the FA/League Cup double

Highbury Stadium evokes the 1930s glory era

Introduction

Arsenal is one of the most legendary names in football: not merely in England but throughout the world. The feats of the Gunners have thrilled not only their local followers in North London but countless millions from Chile to China who have revered the club as a bastion of traditional football authority – and one whose reputation has been reinforced during the Premiership years.

Imaginative thinking has brought the club enormous success down the seasons. It was Sir Henry Norris who originally dared to move the club from one side of the Thames to the other; it was Charlie Buchan and Herbert Chapman who devised a tactical formation which would revolutionize football worldwide; and, most recently, Arsenal have been among the first English clubs to entrust their team to the command of a top foreign coach in Arsène Wenger.

Around and about the club have swirled a galaxy of football's greatest names, and their reward has been to see the club winning League Championships, FA and League Cups and two European trophies in the Cup-Winners' Cup and Inter-Cities Fairs Cup.

Not for Arsenal the messing-about with traditional colours which has made other clubs a laughing-stock. For the Gunners, the immense pride in the red shirts and white shorts has been reciprocated by the loyalty of the fans.

Now, at a time when top clubs are starting to believe that a European super-league may soon be open for business, Arsenal are in the forefront of ambitious development, on and off the pitch.

Highbury itself bears its own magnificent witness: thought by many to be the most impressive stadium in the world it is loved by fans and respected by others. Originally a club from South London, Arsenal made a name for itself in the North of the capital, and has long been one of the South of England's strongest clubs.

Ian Wright's phenomenal strike rate has won him cup medals, England caps and a place in history

Chapter 1

The History of Arsenal

All over the world there are football clubs named after Arsenal, in the hope a little of that magic might rub off. Imitation, they say, is the sincerest form of flattery...

What's in a name?

This is the story of how a works football team, created by a group of Scotsmen outside the Woolwich Arsenal in 1886 with "no name, no pitch and no kit", rose to become the greatest name in world football.

The club formed when 15 men paid twopence halfpenny each to play on Plumstead Common had become the most glamorous club in the world by the 1930s and one of the leading lights in the new competitive Europe by the 1990s.

Arsenal's first trophy in 1930 – the FA Cup – was the beginning of a decade of unparalleled glory for the team which had to beg for its first kit and played its opening match on a pitch bounded by an open sewer.

No one could have been prouder than David Danskin, one of the enterprising young Scotsmen who founded the team for a bit of fun and exercise. The idea had first been raised by two Nottingham Forest players, Fred Beardsley and Morris Bates, who had begun working together at the Woolwich factory. They won their first-ever match 6–0 and decided their name on Christmas Day 1886.

They called themselves Dial Square and then Royal Arsenal – after the Royal Oak pub, in which they held meetings, and their workplace. The colours of red and white were chosen because Beardsley and Bates already had red shirts. A plea to Nottingham Forest from Beardsley produced a whole set of red shirts and a football.

Early matches were played on the only available land – Plumstead Common, an uneven, stony and rutted area used by the Royal Horse Artillery as a training ground. The goalposts were kept in Beardsley's back garden during the week.

Within seven years of their foundation, Woolwich Arsenal, as they then became, were members of the Football League, having won several local championships – most notably the London Charity Cup, a victory over the old boys of Westminster School in front of 10,000 people.

The club first entered the FA Cup, the most prestigious of competitions, as early as 1889–90, winning the first three ties easily, but falling at the first hurdle in the next season.

By this stage, the club had settled down at the Invicta Ground, which had a stand, terraces and dressing-rooms – a vast improvement on the rugged common and sports ground on the old pig farm near Plumstead Marshes where they played until 1888. The Manor Field, which the players grandly nicknamed the Manor Ground, was acquired in haste one February morning after the sports ground was found to be under water hours before a vital match. Players usually changed at one of the local pubs and often had to help collect entrance fees from spectators.

Those days seemed only a distant memory when 12,000 fans turned up at the Invicta on Easter Monday 1891 to watch a game against Scottish champions Hearts. But when the landlord demanded a massive increase in rent – from £250 to £300 a year – hoping to exploit their election to the Football League, the team had to move once again and the old Manor Ground was repurchased.

Arsenal's success proved counter-productive, as several of their best players were lured away by professional clubs. Eventually Arsenal decided that professionalism was the route they must follow as well.

The switch – accomplished along with a change of name from Royal Arsenal to Woolwich Arsenal – provoked their expulsion from the London Association. But that, in turn, spurred the club to turn itself into a limited liability company and help found a second division of the Football League.

When Woolwich Arsenal joined the League in 1893, they were London's only professional club. But apart from two successes in 1906 and 1907, the next 20 years were relatively uneventful for this backwater club from south of the Thames.

Harry Bradshaw took over as secretary-manager at the turn of the century and brought in the two most

Men who mattered: trainer Tom Whittaker, inside-forward Alex James and manager Herbert Chapman

Highbury revolutionary: goalscorer and soccer theorist Charlie Buchan in 1925

notable players of the period; an Australian left-back, Jimmy Jackson, and a new goalkeeper, Jimmy Ashcroft, who became the first Arsenal player to be capped for England.

Results and support improved slowly, the receipts were a healthy £1,000 and in the 1903–04 season they won promotion.

The supporters were well-rewarded in 1906 when the club managed to get past the second round of the FA Cup for the first time and reached the semi-finals, beating Sunderland – four times League champions – by a sensational 5–0 along the way.

A local lad, Charlie Buchan, later wrote that he sold one of his school-books to pay for his admission to the Sunderland game. He could hardly have realised he was watching the two clubs who would dominate most of his spectacular footballing career.

During the next 10 years the more remarkable Arsenal story happened off the field; and all because of a man called Henry Norris, the chairman of Fulham.

The links between the clubs were already close, and in 1910 Norris was able to use the Woolwich club's problems to negotiate a takeover at Arsenal. Norris was Mayor of Fulham for seven years, was knighted in 1917 and was MP for Fulham East from 1918 to 1922. An early property developer from south-east London, he was arrogant and ruthless in both business and football.

After taking over Arsenal, he remained a Fulham director until the First World War. His initial plan was to amalgamate the two teams, move them to Craven Cottage and have a First Division side play there. But the League refused both this and his alternative suggestion, that Fulham and Arsenal could play at Craven Cottage on alternate Saturdays.

He was forced to choose one club and settled on Arsenal. Initially he must have feared he had made the wrong choice, as Arsenal achieved such unenviable records as becoming the first team to win only one home game all season and acquiring the lowest number of points ever recorded in the First Division.

The solution was simple – but drastic. They had to move. Four essential requirements were identified for the new site: it should be within Greater London, in a heavily-populated area not bounded by a river, not too close to another club and easily accessible by public transport.

The solution was a North London site owned by St John's College of Divinity. Arsenal paid a massive £20,000 for a 21-year lease and the deed of transfer was signed by the Archbishop of Canterbury.

To say it was not a popular move is an understatement. The most virulent opposition came from Tottenham Hotspur. They objected, as did Clapton Orient, to Arsenal being within four miles of their club – and so much closer to the vital Underground station. The local residents were none too happy either. It was one thing having a college of divinity on the doorstep, but something else to see it transformed into a football ground.

The last first-class game at the Manor Ground was on Saturday 26 April 1913, and Woolwich Arsenal said goodbye to both their name and south-east London with a 1–1 draw against Middlesbrough.

They became The Arsenal, their public name until Herbert Chapman insisted on a single word being deleted 12 years later (in order to lift them to the top of the Football League alphabet).

Norris began spending lavishly on the new ground. By the time the first match was played at Highbury on 6 September 1913, he had found an astonishing £125,000 – equivalent to around £10 million at today's prices. At the time, Arsenal were a merely a Second Division side – but they won that first game against Leicester Fosse 2–1 and missed promotion only on goal average.

One year later, Europe went to war. By the time it ended, in November 1918, first-class football had effectively ceased to exist – three-quarters of a million young British men had been killed, including a significant number of professional footballers. Yet it was the very confusion created by the interruption of war which offered Norris the opportunity to take Arsenal back into the First Division.

He suggested that the last pre-war season was not quite what it should have been – because of the slide into war – and succeeded in persuading the annual meeting of the Football League that Arsenal, rather than neighbours Tottenham, should be awarded promotion to the First Division.

The Chapman era

The transformation of Arsenal into the greatest club in the land followed the appointment as manager in May 1925 of Herbert Chapman, who had already guided Huddersfield to two League titles. The magnitude of his subsequent achievements is still evident today from the place of honour enjoyed by Chapman's bust

Different era, different standards: in the Thirties smoking was OK for Alex James (second right)

in the marble entrance-halls of the modern Highbury.

On arrival, Chapman warned that it would take five years to build a winning team. His prophecy came true – five years to the week later.

Before his death at 55, Chapman introduced a string of innovations such as the wearing of shirt numbers and floodlit matches. He even persuaded the

Alex James

To many Gunners' fans, Alex James was the greatest player ever to have worn the red and white of Arsenal. Only 5ft 5in in height, the Scot wreaked havoc on opposition sides up and down the country throughout the 1930s.

Alex arrived at Highbury in 1929 from Preston North End, as a direct result of his scintillating performance the previous season when he helped Scotland humiliate England 5–1 in front of a shocked Wembley crowd.

Herbert Chapman recognized genius when he saw it and James became a hero to the Arsenal fans as he turned the Gunners into the world's most famous club, winning four championship medals and two FA Cup winners' medals.

London Electric Railway to change the name of the local Underground station from Gillespie Road to Arsenal.

Chapman also signed the legendary Charlie Buchan in a payment-by-results deal which would not be out of place today. Buchan was playing for Sunderland when Chapman walked into his shop and told him he was signing him for Arsenal – for £2,000 down and £100 for every goal Buchan scored (19).

The Buchan transfer, however, dragged on for weeks because Buchan wanted to be compensated for the likely loss of revenue from his shop. Chapman refused to get involved in this side of the business, leaving everything to Norris, whose over-enthusiasm eventually led him to venture outside the rules and regulations, resulting in his *sine die* suspension over an illegal payments scandal.

Norris was succeeded as chairman by Sir Samuel Hill-Wood, whose family have been involved as directors to this day.

Another historic change was made in October 1925 after a 7–0 defeat by Newcastle. Arsenal's response changed the tactical face of football the world over. Buchan suggested to Chapman that the centre-half should be pulled back to help out in the centre of defence. Thus the so-called third-back game was devised – soon to spread around the world, renowned from its tactical shape as WM.

Chapman's first four seasons were moderately successful and included Arsenal's first appearance in the FA Cup Final, in 1927. It was also the only time the

Cup went out of England. Cardiff City beat favourites Arsenal 1–0 thanks to the slippery new jersey worn by goalkeeper Dan Lewis (a Welshman), a soft shot skidding through his arms.

It was three years before Arsenal returned. When they did, new goalkeeper Charlie Preedy was advised to wear an old, unwashed jersey to avoid a repetition of Lewis's accident.

Four of the original players lived to see that momentous achievement on 26 April 1930, at the Empire Stadium (now known as Wembley), a victory which was broadcast live on the wireless and which was celebrated by both teams (Huddersfield were favourites to win) later that night at the Café Royal.

King George V, recovering from an illness, made his first outdoor appearance for 18 months to preside at the match, which saw both captains come out together for the first time in a major game. It was the beginning of a dream decade for Arsenal, who appeared in two more Cup Finals – in 1932 and 1936, winning the latter – and won five League championships in 1931, 1933, 1934, 1935 and 1938. This was the Arsenal of legend – held in awe at home and renowned throughout the world.

Cliff "Boy" Bastin set a goal-scoring record in 1932–33

Key men included Scotland inside-left Alex James, signed from Preston for £9,000 in 1929 and converted from a goal-poacher into one of the greatest of midfield schemers. Chapman paid £4,000 for flying right winger Joe Hulme in 1926, and the first-ever five-figure fee for inside-right David Jack in 1928, to replace Buchan.

In 1929 he also signed 17-year-old Cliff Bastin from Exeter to partner James on the left wing, and in 1930 Arsenal won that elusive first major honour against Huddersfield in the Cup Final, with goals by James and centre-forward Jack Lambert.

With a defence pivoting on Herbie Roberts, the prototype "stopper" centre-half, and with excellent full-backs in Tom Parker (later succeeded by George Male) and Eddie Hapgood, Arsenal gained a reputation for defensive football.

It was at around this time that the nickname – or complaint – of "Lucky Arsenal" began to be heard around the country. But this was jealousy from opponents caught out by the speed of Arsenal's counter-attacking tactics. James supplied the long, devastating passes, Bastin, Lambert, Jack and Ted Drake the goals. Bastin, for example, scored a record 33 goals from the wing in 1932–33.

Drake set a club record with 42 League goals in 1934–35, and the next season scored seven alone at Villa Park, a First Division record.

This was the Arsenal which secured a hat-trick of League titles from 1933 to 1935. Chapman died after catching pneumonia in 1934, but he left his creation in the capable hands of George Allison, assisted by trainer Tom Whittaker.

Post-War glory

Of course, the world around them was soon changing dramatically. The outbreak of the Second World War in September 1939 saw 42 of the club's 44 professionals drafted into the services. For the players and fans who remained, home was no longer Highbury, now transformed into a base for Air Raid Precautions, but Tottenham's White Hart Lane.

Even so, the Gunners maintained an impressive record of success, winning the South A League (1939–40), the London League (1941–42) and, in 1942–43, both the Football League South and the Football League South Cup Final at Wembley. Four goals from Reg Lewis powered Arsenal's 7–1 rout of Charlton Athletic in that final, and he ended the season with 53 goals.

But football in these years faced many obstacles, not least the high cost. Even immediately after the war, in 1945–46, leagues were organized only on a regional basis, although the FA Cup competition made a welcome return.

The most interesting diversion for Arsenal came, however, with the visit of Soviet side Moscow Dynamo, bringing a taste of foreign excitement and mystery over a decade before regular European competition. Some 56,240 saw Arsenal, including guests such as Stanley Matthews and Stan Mortensen, lose 4–3 in the London fog.

Leading by example: Joe Mercer inspired Arsenal's initial post-war revival

Once regular League football began again the next season, Arsenal reverted to reliance on their own resources – which included two remarkable veterans in 32-year-old Joe Mercer and Ronnie Rooke, 35.

Mercer, an attacking wing-half, had decided to retire and concentrate on his grocery business in Wallasey, but Arsenal's interest persuaded him to make the move from Everton for a fee of £7,000 – even though he did insist on being allowed to live and train in Liverpool.

Rooke, who arrived from Fulham two weeks later, went on to score 21 goals in 24 League games that season, although Lewis was top-scorer, with 29 from 28. After a bad start, a final position of 13th was a

respectable-enough performance, but the Gunners were not content just to be London's top club; somehow they would have to make themselves the country's premier side once more.

Off the pitch, George Allison had retired and trainer Tom Whittaker had taken over as secretary-manager. Whittaker died in 1956, but not before laying the foundations for the long-term health of the club.

The 1947–48 season, Whittaker's first in charge, was one of immediate and spectacular success even without star outside-left Denis Compton, who was busy playing cricket for England. In his absence, his Arsenal team-mates put together a 17-match unbeaten run which ultimately secured the league championship.

The main highlight of the campaign was a 1–1 draw away to title challengers Manchester United at Maine Road in front of 83,260, a Football League record crowd.

Compton returned to duty for the title run-in. He and elder brother Les – Arsenal's centre-half – thus collected League Championship medals to go with their cricket County Championship accolades with Middlesex.

Two years later, it was Arsenal's turn to carry off the FA Cup – the one honour which had previously eluded Mercer, now 35. He played a crucial role in the 2–0 victory over Liverpool in the Final though the meeting made life awkward for the newly-elected Footballer of the Year: after all, Mercer trained daily at Anfield. After the semi-finals, Liverpool allowed him to train only in the afternoons.

In 1951–52, Arsenal came close to the first League

Joe Mercer

Joe Mercer was a tough wing half and inspirational captain who worked in tandem with Tom Whittaker to fill up the Arsenal trophy cabinet.

An England international with Everton, Joe arrived at Highbury at a time when the club, and the country, were still trying to re-build after the trauma of the Second World War.

Arguably Joe's greatest hour came in 1950 when he led Arsenal out at Wembley to face Liverpool in the FA Cup Final. Two goals from Reg Lewis secured the cup for the Gunners.

Although Arsenal lost in the final the following season, Joe led his team to further glory in 1952–53 as the Gunners won the Championship.

Brotherly glory: the FA Cup-winning pride of Denis (left) and Leslie Compton in 1950

and FA Cup double of the century. Disappointment at missing out on both prizes was amply offset by championship success the following season. Arsenal's seventh title was then a record, its achievement owing much to the veteran Scotland inside-forward Jimmy Logie. Only two other regulars from 1948 remained in support: Mercer and Roper.

Mercer's career came to an unhappy end in April 1954, when he broke a leg playing against Liverpool, but as one player departed, another emerged: that same game saw young Welsh forward Derek Tapscott, signed from Barry Town, score two goals on his debut. The overall pattern of the season, however, was set by a humiliating 7–1 defeat at Sunderland, goalkeeper George Swindin's last game for the club.

Tom Whittaker's death on October 24, 1956, changed everything. The tributes paid to him reflected the high regard in which he had been held – not only for his management skills but also for the good humour he invariably brought to his activities. As Mercer said: "He never did a bad thing. All problems had only one solution: the one done with kindness."

The solution the Arsenal directors hoped would restore the club's fortunes was to split the secretary-manager job into two positions, installing Bob Wall as secretary, and former Arsenal star Jack Crayston as manager.

Crayston had won two League Championships and the 1936 FA Cup as a player at the club, but his stint as manager, which began in December 1956, brought nothing, despite the emergence of the likes of inside-forward Vic Groves and centre-forward David Herd. The board's reluctance to compete at the top end of the transfer market did not help, and Crayston resigned in the summer of 1958, to be succeeded by ex-goalkeeper Swindin.

His first season, when Arsenal finished third, proved to be the peak of his managerial achievements at Highbury. The purchase of the Scottish duo Tommy Docherty and Jackie Henderson brought a glimmer of enthusiasm and excitement but the record £50,000 purchase of Mel Charles was a failure.

Building for the future

In 1961 the season ended as it had done a decade earlier, with Arsenal's shortcomings standing in sharp contrast to the title-winning credentials of rivals Tottenham – only this time, Spurs were creating history by becoming the first club this century to win the League and FA Cup double.

It was not until 10 years later that Arsenal would emulate this achievement. In the meantime, Swindin was replaced as manager by England legend Billy Wright in the summer of 1962.

Wright's arrival was accompanied by a new coach – Les Shannon – and a new striking partnership, Joe Baker (signed for £70,000 from Torino) and Geoff Strong. Between them they scored 52 goals in 1962–63, and 57 in 1963–64. However, Arsenal continued to have problems at the other end of the pitch, their leaky defence condemning them to mid-table disappointment throughout Wright's time in charge.

Wright recognized himself as too inexperienced to solve the club's obvious problems. Geoff Strong was sold to Bill Shankly's Liverpool in November 1964, after impressing in the first match screened on BBC TV's Match of the Day, a 2–2 draw between Arsenal and Liverpool at Highbury.

The 1965–66 season was Wright's Arsenal swan-song; a final spot of 14th place was the club's worst showing since 1930. Wright's sacking was inevitable, and it was confirmed once he had returned from his involvement in BBC's coverage of the 1966 World Cup finals.

Yet Wright had not wasted his time in charge. The youngsters had won the FA Youth Cup in 1965–66, boasting a line-up including future first-teamers Pat Rice and Sammy Nelson. Wright had also given debuts to Peter Simpson, John Radford and Bob Wilson, and recruited the services of centre-half Frank McLintock, all of whom would play crucial roles in the 1970–71 triumphs.

In April 1964, Wright had brought Don Howe to the club, signing the international defender from West Bromwich Albion. Howe would go on – as coach – to mastermind the tactics of the double success.

But it was a low-key appointment made in the summer of 1960 which would have the most significant bearing on the Gunners' future success: as the club moved their training facilities from Highbury and Hendon to London Colney, they also appointed a new physiotherapist. Six years later, that physiotherapist became Arsenal's new manager, and Bertie Mee launched the Arsenal revival.

The decision to promote Mee came as a surprise to many, who had expected Wright to be replaced with another high-profile name.

But in his six years at Highbury, Mee had built a reputation within the club as an effective organizer and authoritarian. His role as physio had brought him into regular contact with the players, and had developed in him a keen sense of how the side should be

Cup Final, 1972: Dynamic duo Peter Simpson and Frank McLintock overpower Leeds' Mick Jones

reshaped. Twenty years of experience in running FA injury courses and lecturing managers and coaches at Lilleshall also bore witness to Mee's experience and knowledge of the game.

However, he partly shared the feeling that this was merely a temporary appointment. Mee came to an agreement with the board that if, after 12 months, things were not working out, he could return to his previous position.

This personal pragmatism was immediately applied to the club as a whole. According to Mee: "There was nothing immediately wrong but the club had to be more professional from all angles. The danger was that mediocrity was being perpetuated."

Mee's first moves were to bring in Dave Sexton as his new coach, and then to withdraw Arsenal from the Metropolitan League. Not only did this cut costs but also focused the club's attention on the League and Cup commitments which really mattered.

From then on, the advances made towards the double of 1970–71 were steadily impressive. A top-half finish in Mee's first year in charge was a reasonable achievement and although Sexton left for Chelsea – to be replaced as coach by Don Howe – the Gunners reached the League Cup Final in the 1967–68 season. A controversial goal by Leeds' Terry Cooper denied Mee

George Armstrong

Armstrong was brought to Highbury in 1961 from the north-eastern team Hebburn. He was a fast and fearless left winger and he made a then record 500 appearances for the Gunners before he left to play for Leicester in 1977. He was a member of the Inter-Cities Fairs cup winning team that beat Anderlecht in the final in 1970. Armstrong was tireless in attack and could always be relied upon to come back to defend if necessary. Although he earned himself 23 caps at England under-23 level, it was surprising and sad that the deserving player was never picked by either Sir Alf Ramsey or Don Revie at senior level.

Safety first: Star goalkeeper-turned-television soccer presenter Bob Wilson

his first trophy, but the signs were that Arsenal could expect more Wembley visits in the coming years.

What was most significant about Mee's Arsenal was his restoration of the trademark defensive solidity which had alarmingly deserted the club in the late 1950s and early 1960s. With Bob Wilson emerging as a formidably brave and reliable goalkeeper, and captain Frank McLintock marshalling the back line with authority, Mee was constructing the side on secure foundations.

This is why it came as such a shock when, having reached the League Cup Final for the second successive year, Arsenal collapsed 3–1 to Third Division Swindon Town. The players were not helped by terrible conditions at Wembley, where heavy rainfall had affected the pitch. Ironically, the Swindon debâcle may have aroused the avenging spirit which helped the club edge towards the double.

The double and European triumph

The 1969–70 season brought the first tangible evidence of Mee's success in rebuilding the club, with victory in the Fairs Cup. It was the Gunners' first trophy in 17 years and provided a triumphant climax to a season which had seen debuts up-front for Charlie George and Ray Kennedy, as well as the much-hyped arrival from Hibernian of the flamboyant Peter Marinello.

But it was the 1970–71 season which eclipsed all other achievements.

Ten years after Tottenham had become the first side this century to win the League and Cup double, there were not many people who believed the feat would be repeated, least of all by Arsenal.

The partnership of John Radford and 19-year-old Kennedy, supported by George and the more experienced George Graham, were beginning to produce the steady stream of goals which turned Arsenal into genuine title contenders, fit to compete with pre-season favourites Leeds, Chelsea and reigning champions Everton.

A fourth-round defeat by Crystal Palace ended Arsenal's League Cup ambitions, but greater things were soon to come. Mee's reaction to disappointing displays was uncompromising but guaranteed to get the best out of his players.

Graham had been switched from attack to midfield, where his stylish skills and poise added a touch of flair

Charlie George

Charlie George lived out every schoolboy's dream. Born in nearby Holloway, as a child he was a regular in the North Bank and by the age of 19 he was a star in the team. His skills were dazzling – a great example is his drilling pinpoint shot won Arsenal the FA Cup Final in 1971 – but his discipline let him down. George was erratic as a player and was also let down by injuries. He played only 133 League games for the Gunners in six seasons and when Derby County paid £90,000 for him in 1976 he seemed pleased to move, but Charlie George will always be remembered by adoring Arsenal fans.

to the Arsenal side, and his consistent ability to weigh in with his share of goals was a major benefit.

As the season progressed, however, it looked more and more likely that Leeds would be crowned champions for the second time in three years, Don Revie's side possessing the advantage of points in the bag, rather than games in hand. As Arsenal progressed in the FA Cup, the pressures of fixture congestion became ever-greater for Mee and his men – ironically, a problem which had fatally hampered Leeds' title challenge the previous season.

Arsenal entered April 1971 with their double ambitions hanging by a fine thread. At half-time in the FA Cup semi-final against Stoke, Arsenal trailed 2–0. But two goals from rugged midfielder Peter Storey – the

Double delight: Charlie George rose from terrace fan to title-winner

second in injury time – earned a replay which saw Arsenal run out 2–0 winners, with goals from Graham and Kennedy.

That recovery revitalized Arsenal for the closing stages of the League battle. They lost 1–0 away to Leeds but, by the time the season reached its climax, the fate of the championship was in the Gunners' own hands.

Leeds had already completed their season but Arsenal's progress in the FA Cup had meant the rescheduling of their final game to the Monday evening before the Cup Final.

The mathematics of the League table meant that if Arsenal won, they were champions; if they lost, the crown went to Leeds. The issue was complicated by the fact that Arsenal could hold out for a goalless draw and finish top but, if they were involved in a scoring draw, the goal average calculations would work in Leeds's favour.

Just to add more spice and interest to this climax to the season, Arsenal's opponents were North London rivals Tottenham – and the fixture was to be played at White Hart Lane.

A crowd of 51,192 had to wait until the 87th minute to witness the decisive goal from Ray Kennedy.

Arsenal were thus not only champions for a record eighth time but they were about to emulate the achievement of their North London rivals.

Liverpool, their Cup Final opponents, were the Wembley favourites. Yet Bill Shankly's side were unable to raise their game sufficiently until the second minute of extra time, when Steve Heighway raced clear to shoot past Bob Wilson.

This was the cue for George Graham to push further forward into the Arsenal attack, and his presence proved significant minutes later in producing the equalizer after a shot from Eddie Kelly.

It was Charlie George, a terrace supporter as a boy, who would go down in history as the man who secured Arsenal's glory with just nine minutes left on the referee's watch. Thus Mee had achieved something which had even eluded Herbert Chapman in the 1930s.

Mee's Arsenal boasted relatively few established internationals and lacked the glamour and flair of Tottenham's double-winning side. But when it came down to teamwork and determination, this Arsenal team were second to none.

Anything would have been an anti-climax after the spectacular and, to many, surprising glory of the 1970–71 season. But in the summer of 1971, the cracks were already beginning to appear. Howe was tempted away by the manager's job at West Bromwich Albion, taking with him George Wright and youth team coach Brian Whitehouse. Steve Burtenshaw was appointed as Howe's replacement but the momentum of the previous season was lost, and the side proved too inconsistent to retain their hold on the twin titles.

Turbulent times

The signing of Alan Ball from Everton in December 1971, for a British record £220,000, helped the side stage a mini-revival which fell just short of winning a UEFA Cup place but the chance of consolation came when the Gunners again reached the FA Cup Final, in the competition's centenary year.

Again, it was a drab game which disappointed the Wembley spectators, but this time it was Arsenal who fell victim to a late goal, scored for Leeds by Allan Clarke.

A 2–1 defeat by Second Division Sunderland prevented Arsenal reaching the FA Cup Final for a third consecutive season; and with the Gunners finishing runners-up to League Champions Liverpool, Mee needed to do something to reinvigorate the club. McLintock joined QPR and George Graham departed for Manchester United, while Burtenshaw resigned as coach, to be replaced by Bobby Campbell. More disruptive was the loss of form suffered by Ray Kennedy, who was eventually sold to Liverpool for £200,000. His replacement, Manchester United's Brian Kidd, lasted only two years at Arsenal, without making a great impact.

Discontent among the players also contributed to Arsenal's decline, with Ball putting in a transfer request and losing the captaincy at the start of the 1975–76 season. The club dipped worryingly close to the bottom of the table, and Peter Storey's abrupt 10-day walk-out in March encapsulated the frustration and ill-feeling sweeping Highbury. Perhaps this was the final straw for Mee, who announced his decision to retire at the end of the season, bringing to an end a 10-year reign which had hit the heights, but which was now threatening to sink to the depths.

Despite losing their final three games, the Gunners just managed to avoid relegation to the Second Division.

A lobby of the club's players, including Ball, Armstrong and Terry Mancini, wanted Campbell to be promoted as Mee's successor, but the job was eventually offered to Arsenal old boy Terry Neill, who had

been in charge at Tottenham. Neill brought with him Wilf Dixon as his assistant – signalling Campbell's Highbury exit. Not surprisingly, the outspoken Ball was soon on his way out too, joining Southampton in a £60,000 deal.

Neill's first major signing brought an instant injection of charisma to the club; he secured the services of Malcolm Macdonald from Newcastle for £333,333, despite competition for the signing from Tottenham. Supermac hit 29 goals in his first season at Highbury and gave the club and the supporters, a much-needed boost.

There had been signs in Mee's final months at the club that brighter times were on the horizon. Most significant was the emergence of three talented young Irishmen – centre-back David O'Leary, midfielder Liam Brady and striker Frank Stapleton.

The first chance for Neill to get his hands on some silverware came when Arsenal reached the 1978 FA Cup Final. The 1977–78 season had begun with Howe returning to Highbury as coach and goalkeeper Pat Jennings, then with Spurs, making the short journey across North London for £40,000. Both were undoubtedly key figures in the Gunners' march back to Wembley. Having lost in the League Cup semi-final to Liverpool, Arsenal were determined to capture the FA Cup and win their first trophy for seven years, but Bobby Robson's Ipswich caused an upset by winning 1–0.

Arsenal were severely hampered by fitness problems, with Rice, Nelson, Young, Macdonald, Brady and Sunderland all carrying injuries which affected their performances, but Neill was confident that they could come back and win the trophy next time.

Which is precisely what they did, although in circumstances no one, least of all Neill, could have foreseen. Arsenal looked as if they were coasting to victory over Manchester United, goals from Brian Talbot and Frank Stapleton giving them a 2–0 lead with five minutes left to play. It was then that the Final sprang into life. United scored twice to level the match, then Alan Sunderland shot Arsenal's winner. It came to be known as the Five-Minute Final.

Liam Brady's emergence in the second half of the 1970s had established him as one of the most exciting talents in Arsenal's history. His exquisite poise was made even more enthralling by the seemingly magical control exerted by his left foot, which was admiringly referred to as "The Claw". But Brady dismayed Arsenal fans by announcing that the 1979–80 season would be his last at the club before he left to play abroad.

Power play: Arsenal striker Ray Kennedy out-paces Chelsea's David Webb

Liam Brady

Liam Brady broke into the Arsenal first team in 1973, having signed for the Gunners as an apprentice, and for the seven years that followed, he proved to be such a midfield great that many believed that he could never be replaced. Brady was born in Dublin and played for his country at junior and senior level. He teamed up perfectly with David O'Leary and Frank Stapleton, fellow juniors with whom Brady battled his way to three consecutive FA Cup finals in the 1970s. In 1980, Juventus paid £600,000 for him and he ended his Highbury playing career after 235 League appearances and 43 goals.

It would have been fitting if Brady could have signed out with another winners' medal. But he was to be thwarted on two fronts. After overcoming Liverpool in an epic four-match semi-final tie, Arsenal became the first club this century to reach a third consecutive FA Cup Final – only to lose to West Ham. In the Cup-winners' Cup, they lost to Valencia in a penalty shoot-out.

The departures of Brady to Juventus in 1980 and Stapleton to Manchester United in 1981 effectively consigned Arsenal to the ranks of the also-rans for much of the 1980s. They finished third, fifth, 10th and sixth in the first four seasons of the 1980s, and their failure to sustain a realistic title challenge was compounded by humiliating Cup defeats.

A 2–1 Milk Cup defeat at home to Walsall in November 1983 was the last straw for frustrated Arsenal fans, who were becoming increasingly desperate the club's League failures, despite the expensive signings of £650,000 Charlie Nicholas and £500,000 Tommy Caton. After subsequent losses at West Brom and West Ham, Neill was sacked, and Don Howe finally fulfilled his ambition to manage the club, albeit initially on a caretaker basis.

Howe failed, however, to avoid the kind of embarrassing Cup exits which had contributed to Neill's downfall. Second Division Oxford sent the Gunners tumbling out of the Milk Cup, while their FA Cup campaign came to an ignominious end at Fourth Division York City.

The club's centenary season, 1985–86, was not much better, the side's efforts falling apart with Milk Cup defeat at the quarter-final stage to Aston Villa, quickly followed by a 3–0 defeat at Luton in an FA Cup fifth-round replay. In March 1986 Arsenal hit a new nadir when Howe asked to be released from his contract.

The stage was then set for the suave, stylish George Graham to stroll back into Highbury on 15 May, 1986, having spent four years in charge of Millwall. In true Highbury tradition, Arsenal were looking to the future by keeping in touch with the club's history. As the club embarked on its second century, the man who had tasted Arsenal triumph as a player in 1971 was about to lead his old club to greater glory as manager.

Graham's immediate success on his return to Highbury was all the more fascinating in that he refused to splash out on expensive signings, preferring to consider and assess the staff already at the club.

This faith meant promising youngsters at the club were given a chance to shine which they might not otherwise have received – with gratifying results. It was during Howe's time in charge that young players such as Tony Adams, David Rocastle and Niall Quinn had made their first-team debuts. But it was under Graham that these players began to flourish.

Two more Championships

The 1987 Littlewoods Cup Final against Liverpool provided Graham with his first trophy as Arsenal manager. When Ian Rush scored for Liverpool midway through the first half, it seemed all over; after all, Liverpool had never lost a game in which Rush had scored. With this his last Wembley appearance before leaving for Juventus, it seemed inevitable that he would leave with a winners' medal.

But Arsenal's tradition of accomplishing the unpredictable comeback was to supply another glory-story, thanks to one of the most unpredictable players in the club's recent history: Charlie Nicholas.

Nicholas arrived from Celtic in 1983 in a fusillade of hype. Like Peter Marinello a decade earlier, he arrived in London touting a reputation as a long-haired, flamboyant playboy promising to bring glitz and glamour to a dour Arsenal side. The reality was that, like Marinello, his performances often fell short of the promise. At Wembley on 5 April 1987, however, "Champagne Charlie" was justifiably the man to lead the Arsenal celebrations, scoring two goals – the winner eight minutes from time – to cap Graham's memorable first season.

The following season Arsenal returned to Wembley to defend the Littlewoods Cup; but whereas they had upset the odds with a late winner to beat Liverpool, they found the tables turned on them by Luton Town. Goals from Martin Hayes and Alan Smith had put the Gunners into a 2–1 lead with eight minutes remaining. It was then that Gunners left-back Nigel Winterburn had a penalty saved by Luton keeper Andy Dibble, and within a minute Danny Wilson had equalized. Seconds remained when Brian Stein struck again to break Arsenal's grip on the trophy.

Arsenal finished the League season in sixth place, but there were few signs to suggest they would end up as champions the next time around. While other clubs had been splashing out on increasingly-expensive signings, Graham had kept his chequebook in his pocket, except to pay a modest £400,000 each for the little-known full-backs Winterburn and Lee Dixon to replace Sansom and Anderson.

It was a slump in form in March 1989, threatening to imperil Arsenal's position at the top of the table, which motivated Graham to first experiment with his formation. Discarding the traditional back-four strategy, he employed David O'Leary as a sweeper behind Steve Bould and Tony Adams, allowing Dixon and Winterburn to push up on the wings and Rocastle to adopt a more attacking attitude in midfield.

The Hillsborough tragedy in April cast a pall over the season, creating confusion as to how events would develop. Liverpool's vital League game with Arsenal at Anfield was postponed, among others, and Arsenal decided to postpone their next game as well.

When the season resumed, victories over Norwich and Middlesbrough were followed by defeat at home to Derby and a draw at home to Wimbledon. Victories for Liverpool in their next games put the Anfield side three points clear with just one game left – when Arsenal would have to travel to Liverpool and come away with a win by two goals to snatch the title on goal difference.

That Arsenal should have pulled off such a feat was remarkable. That they scored the second, crucial goal when the game had entered injury time was a dramatic end to the League season which could have been taken straight out of a Roy of the Rovers story.

The pressure applied to the Liverpool goal was relentless, but, despite Alan Smith's 52nd-minute goal it looked as if the Liverpool defence would survive to clinch an unprecedented second League and Cup double. The clock had already passed the 90-minute mark when Alan Smith helped Dixon's clearance on to Michael Thomas, who somehow raced through Steve Nicol and Ray Houghton before prodding the ball decisively past Grobbelaar into the Liverpool net.

Amazingly, the championship was no longer Liverpool's but Arsenal's, for the first time since Graham had been a part of the double-winning side.

After the euphoria of the title triumph, it was in keeping with Arsenal tradition that the next season was a comparative let-down. The club finished fourth as the title returned to Liverpool, and both domestic Cup campaigns ended in fourth-round defeats. The ban on English clubs in European competition was still in force, so Arsenal were denied the opportunity to compete in the European Champions' Cup.

For 1990–91, Graham again managed to achieve a perfect balance between team continuity and the necessary signing of new players. The nucleus remained constant from the 1989 triumph but two crucial additions were made: in the close season of 1990, Graham

David O'Leary

David O'Leary was the personification of all that is good about Arsenal.

Loyal, hard-working and totally committed, the Irishman spent 20 years at Highbury during which time he racked up a staggering 722 appearances for the Gunners, including 558 League matches.

As a solid, dependable defender, David had few, if any equals, during the 1980s when he was at the peak of his considerable powers.

paid £1.3 million for QPR's David Seaman, then a British record for a goalkeeper, before parting with another £1 million to sign Swede Anders Limpar from Italy's Cremonese. A reliable goalkeeper and an exciting goal-provider were the two crucial ingredients which brought the title back to Highbury: Limpar's blistering start to the season gave Arsenal the perfect lift-off, and he ended the season having scored 11 goals and created many more. Seaman enjoyed a remarkable season in the Arsenal goal, conceding a mere 18 goals.

His one off-day came in April, when Arsenal and Tottenham were drawn together for the first-ever FA

Cup semi-final to be contested by the two North London rivals. The FA made the unprecedented decision to stage the match at Wembley, but that was to be Arsenal's only visit to the Twin Towers that season – a stunning free-kick from Paul Gascoigne after only two minutes and two goals from Gary Lineker condemned Arsenal to a painful 3–1 defeat.

But while Spurs were on their way to FA Cup triumph, their North London rivals were making sure of the League Championship. It was on 19 January that Arsenal climbed to pole position, and after a 2–1 defeat at Chelsea on 2 February, Graham's men remained unbeaten for the rest of the League season. The title was clinched on May 6 when the Gunners celebrated with a 3–1 win over Manchester United. Alan Smith scored all three and ended the season as top-scorer with 23 goals. Another hat-trick came on the last day of the season, this time from Limpar, in a 6–1 rout of Coventry.

What made Arsenal's success, and the unshakeable consistency behind it, the more praiseworthy was the series of unexpected setbacks (at times self-inflicted) suffered during the season.

The first came on 20 October in an explosive fixture at Manchester United, when every player on the pitch, excluding Seaman, became involved in a mass brawl, for which Arsenal were docked two points and Manchester United one point by the FA: both clubs were also fined £50,000.

When they met again in November, in a Rumbelows Cup tie at Highbury, United stunned the Gunners with a 6–2 win. For a team which had only just equalled a club record of 17 games without defeat and had recently gone 602 minutes without conceding a goal, this was an inexplicable setback.

When club captain Tony Adams was jailed for drink-driving in December, it seemed that Arsenal's season was cursed. Adams missed a total of eight League games, during which time Andy Linighan, signed from Norwich, deputized competently.

In Adams's absence, Arsenal actually moved to the top of the First Division for the first time that season – and when the inspirational skipper was restored to the side, there was little chance of the Gunners letting their lead slip. Even Liverpool, the defending champions, proved incapable of living up to the challenge.

The season ended with North London triumphant; Arsenal League Champions, Tottenham FA Cup-winners. The Charity Shield meeting between the two sides ended, predictably, in a goalless draw. Mirroring the

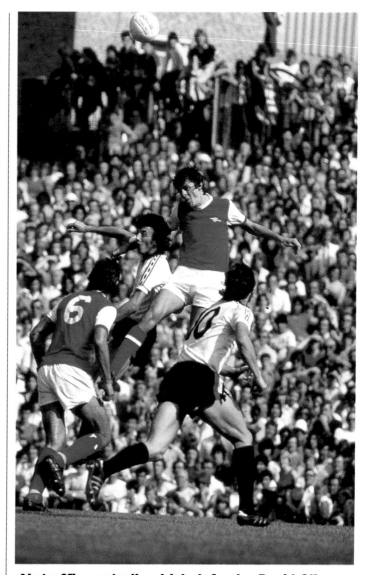

Air traffic controller: Irish defender David O'Leary clears the lines against Bristol City

pattern set two seasons earlier, Arsenal followed up their title-winning campaign by finishing fourth.

Graham's solid structure was starting to wobble. Smith could no longer supply enough goals, Graham had lost faith in the erratic Limpar and youngsters such as Campbell, Hillier and Parlour were still finding their first-team feet.

Now, at last, Graham splashed out on an expensive, high-profile signing to ignite the side and the fans – in the shape of Ian Wright, purchased from Crystal Palace for £2.5 million in September.

Wright made a typically explosive start. He hit a hat-trick on his Arsenal debut in a 4–0 win at Southampton and ended his first season in Arsenal colours as top scorer in the First Division – the last player to win that award, as the top flight metamorphosed into the Premier League.

The Premiership Years

As the last team to win the League Championship, Arsenal have yet to win the new-look title. Instead, success has come in cup competitions and Europe

THE LAST pre-Premiership English season was not notable only by virtue of being the last time the first division really was the First Division.

When Leeds United captured their first championship in 18 years, fighting off a challenge from Manchester United, it marked the end of the dominant Liverpool-Arsenal axis which had produced title triumphs for Liverpool in 1988 and 1990, and for Arsenal in 1989 and 1991. For the first time in five years, neither of these two sides was to be crowned champions – and neither has been since.

If one team has dominated the Premiership 1990s, it has undoubtedly been Manchester United – and the overwhelming dominance of Alex Ferguson's side has only served to bring into starker relief the relative failures of the other two sides in red.

Arsenal have, at least, enjoyed more success in the cup competitions than Liverpool, or indeed, any other English side (except, perhaps, United) – but there is no doubt that many Arsenal fans harbour lingering disappointments that the title wins of 1989 and 1991 were not the beginnings of a new Arsenal era – particularly when the advent of the Premiership launched English

Arsène Wenger has revived Arsenal's title hopes with new tactics and a string of foreign signings

league football into a brave new world.

Now, with Arsène Wenger's first season at the club having brought the first realistic title challenge since George Graham was successful in 1991, Highbury must be optimistic about the prospect of an Arsenal captain raising the championship trophy in triumph. While the Premiership era may not have brought Arsenal a further title, however, it has provided a wealth of ups and downs for the club, with glittering success on the field accompanied by frenzied upheaval: the 1990s have assuredly seen Arsenal shake off their "boring" tag, both in footballing and non-footballing terms.

The new era opened, appropriately enough, with a new foreign signing, setting a pattern which Arsene Wenger would subsequently embellish.

1992–93

14 JULY John Jensen, fresh from winning a European Championship medal with Denmark, joins from Brondby for £1.1 million.

23 JULY Highbury hero David Rocastle, one of the big successes of the club's youth system, is surprisingly sold to Leeds United for £2 million.

15 AUG The opening day of the season starts well but ends disastrously, as Arsenal waste a 2–0 lead to suffer a 4–2 home defeat at the hands of Norwich City.

23 AUG Anders Limpar and Ian Wright score the goals at Liverpool to give the Gunners their first points of the season.

3 SEPT The club drops its all-ticket policy in response to below-average attendances. Just 23,000 attended the previous 2–1 home win over Sheffield Wednesday.

7 OCT David Seaman saves three penalties to scrape past first-division Millwall in a Coca-Cola Cup second-round shoot-out after two 1–1 draws.

7 NOV Spurs do their North London rivals a favour by winning at leaders Blackburn, meaning that the Gunners go top for the first time this season, after their sixth win in succession: 3–0 against Coventry.

16 DEC Ian Wright is charged with misconduct after punching Tottenham's David Howells in the previous Saturday's fiery North London derby.

30 DEC Former Gunner Jack Crayston, who played for the club in the 1930s and returned as manager in the 1950s, dies at 82.

2 JAN Ian Wright's hat-trick eases the Gunners past non-league Yeovil in the FA Cup third round.

4 JAN In further fall-out from December's derby against Spurs, George Graham is charged with misconduct for remarks made to match officials.

6 JAN Nigel Winterburn defies fog to strike the only goal at Scarborough in the Coca-Cola Cup quarter-final tie.

7 JAN Wright is banned for three matches after TV evidence the Howells incident, while Graham is fined £500 for his post-match remarks to referee Alf Buksh.

Anders Limpar rifles home the first goal in a 2–0 win against Liverpool at Anfield. After scoring only one more goal for Arsenal in 1992–93, Limpar returned to Merseyside to join Everton in 1994

Martin Keown's return to Highbury in 1993 for £2 million helped the versatile defender win back his place in the England team

25 JAN Arsenal pull off one of their customary comeback tricks. Paul Merson grabs a late equalizer to secure a 2–2 FA Cup draw at League Champions Leeds and send the sides back to Highbury.

31 JAN A nightmare performance at home sees the Gunners miss their fourth penalty of the season, Nigel Winterburn is sent off, and struggling Liverpool carry a 1–0 win back to Merseyside.

1 FEB Martin Keown returns to Highbury in a £2 million move from Everton – seven years after Graham released him to Villa for a paltry £200,000.

3 FEB Another late, late show in the FA Cup, as Leeds take the Gunners to extra time before losing the replay showdown 3–2: predictably, Wright scores the winner, his second of the game

7 FEB Palace old-boy Wright scores Arsenal's opener in the Coca-Cola Cup semi-final first leg at Selhurst Park, on the way to a 3–1 win.

27 FEB Club captain Tony Adams needs 29 stitches to a head wound after falling down a flight of stairs.

6 MAR A 4–2 win at Ipswich puts Arsenal through to the FA Cup semi-finals, where the club will again meet Spurs at Wembley, for the second time in three years.

10 MAR Ian Wright and Andy Linighan complete a 5–1 aggregate win over Palace in the Coca-Cola Cup semi-finals.

19 MAR Arsenal reveal that David O'Leary will leave on a free transfer at the end of the season, ending an 18-year Highbury career.

4 APR A late headed winner from Tony Adams brings revenge for 1991 as Arsenal beat Tottenham to reach their second domestic final of the season. Lee Dixon is sent off late in the game, however, and will miss the Coca-Cola Cup Final.

Cup Kings: Arsenal became the first side to win the League Cup and FA Cup in the same year

6 APR David Hillier is ruled out of the Coca-Cola Cup final after suffering ligament injuries in a 1–0 defeat by bottom-of-the-table Middlesbrough.

18 APR The Gunners win the Coca-Cola Cup after a second-half winner from unlikely hero Steve Morrow – who later breaks an arm when the post-match celebrations go wrong

22 APR Ian Wright breaks a toe, and raises concerns about his fitness for the FA Cup final.

6 MAY 18 days after the Coca-Cola Cup game, and nine days before the FA Cup final, the League encounter between Arsenal and Sheffield Wednesday ends in a 1–0 victory for Trevor Francis' side.

8 MAY Wright resoundingly proves his fitness, scoring a hat-trick to send his old Palace team-mates down into the First Division.

11 MAY An under-strength Arsenal side goes down 3–1 at home to Tottenham.

15 MAY A disappointing FA Cup Final ends in a 1–1 draw, Ian Wright scoring the Arsenal goal before David Hirst nets an equalizer.

18 MAY Arsenal announce plans to install two giant video screens at Highbury next season.

20 MAY Andy Linighan earns himself a place in Arsenal history, heading a 119th-minute winner to complete a historic cup double for the Gunners. George Graham becomes the first man to win all three domestic titles as both player and manager.

Strutting their stuff: Kevin Campbell celebrates his second goal of Arsenal's 4–0 win over Swindon with Ian Wright.

28 MAY Both Arsenal and Sheffield Wednesday are disciplined by the FA for fielding under-strength line-ups in the Premier League games running up to the FA Cup final.

29 MAY Ian Wright scores his first goal in an England shirt, hitting a late equalizer in the World Cup qualifier in Poland.

5 JUNE Tony Adams and David Seaman pull out of England's squad for the US Cup '93, both due to undergo hernia operations.

1993–94

7 AUG Ian Wright and David Seaman miss penalties as Manchester United win the Charity Shield, after a 1–1 draw takes the match to a shoot-out.

14 AUG Coventry striker Mick Quinn stuns Arsenal with a hat-trick, as the Sky Blues win 3–0 at Highbury.

16 AUG Ian Wright scores an 87th-minute winner to clinch a tight North London derby at White Hart Lane.

11 SEPT Kevin Campbell hits a spectacular hat-trick in a 4–0 trouncing of Ipswich, taking the Gunners level with League leaders Manchester United.

15 SEPT Odense take an early lead in the first round, first leg of the Cup-winners' Cup, but goals from Wright and Merson give Arsenal a 2–1 lead to take back to Highbury.

19 SEPT Eric Cantona scores the only goal in the top-of-the-table clash between Manchester United and Arsenal at Old Trafford.

21 SEPT Ian Wright scores a hat-trick as Huddersfield are beaten 5–0 in the Coca-Cola Cup.

29 SEPT An unconvincing 1–1 draw with Odense at Highbury is enough to take Arsenal into the second round of the Cup-winners' Cup.

20 OCT Two more goals from Ian Wright, and another from Paul Merson, effectively end Standard Liège's interest in the Cup-winners' Cup.

30 OCT Stalemate with Norwich means October has been a month of four successive goalless draws in the Premiership.

3 NOV Arsenal run riot in Belgium, hitting seven without reply against a shell-shocked Standard Liège side to complete a 10–0 aggregate win.

10 NOV The Gunners win 3–0 at Norwich to book their place in the fourth round of the Coca-Cola Cup; Wright scores two of the goals, with Merson adding the other.

17 NOV Wright scores four goals in England's 7–1 win over San Marino, but it is not enough to qualify for the 1994 World Cup in America.

20 NOV Alan Smith and Ian Wright, with a penalty, grab the goals to secure a win over Chelsea at Stamford Bridge. Arsenal are yet to be beaten by any London rival.

30 NOV Arsenal's hold on the Coca-Cola Cup is ended as Aston Villa inflict the Gunners' first defeat in 26 Cup ties. Andy Townsend scores the only goal at Highbury.

8 DEC The Highbury pitch is deemed four metres too short to stage matches at Euro 96.

27 DEC Kevin Campbell enjoys a post-Christmas treat, smashing a hat-trick as bottom-club Swindon are beaten 4–0.

10 JAN Arsenal kick off their defence of the FA Cup with a 1–0 win over Millwall, courtesy of Tony Adams's last-minute goal.

9 FEB First-division Bolton win 3–1 at Highbury, after extra time, to end the holders' involvement in this year's FA Cup competition.

28 FEB Neither Ian Wright, Paul Merson nor Lee Dixon is included in Terry Venables's first England squad.

2 MAR Some typically stout defending means Arsenal return from their Cup-winners' Cup quarter-final game against Torino with a goalless draw.

15 MAR Tony Adams scores the only goal at Highbury as Torino are eliminated, and Arsenal are through to the Cup-Winners' Cup semi-finals.

29 MAR Arsenal score an early away goal against Paris St. Germain, Wright giving them a first-half lead, although David Ginola later equalizes for the French side.

12 APR Kevin Campbell scores after just five minutes in the Cup-Winners' Cup semi-final second leg, a goal which is enough to take Arsenal into the final, although Wright is ruled out of that match after his second booking of the tournament.

20 APR John Jensen is also ruled out of the final, picking up an injury in Denmark's 3–1 win over Hungary.

30 APR The Gunners lose their first Premiership game in 20, in a 2–0 derby defeat by West Ham.

4 MAY Alan Smith's goal is enough to defeat holders Parma in the Cup-Winners' Cup final and give the club their first European trophy in 24 years.

7 MAY On the League season's last day Arsenal-reject Andy Cole scores a record 41st goal of the season as Newcastle beat the Gunners 2–0, meaning Newcastle finish third and Arsenal fourth.

1 JUNE Swedish World Cup midfielder Stefan Schwarz signs from Benfica for £1.75 million.

1994–95

14 JUNE Arsenal pull out of the two-club chase for £5 million Chris Sutton, allowing Blackburn to sign the striker from Norwich.

5 AUG The club announce record profits of £5.63 million for a turnover of £21.5 million: for the first time, commercial profits overtake gate receipts.

7 AUG New boy Stefan Schwarz is voted Player of the Tournament, as Arsenal clinch the pre-season Makita Cup with a 1–0 win over Napoli.

28 AUG Liverpool's Robbie Fowler hits a hat-trick in record time, as Arsenal lose 3–0 at Anfield.

15 SEPT Arsenal kick off their defence of the Cup-Winners' Cup with a 3–1 win in Cyprus over Omonia Nicosia, Merson netting twice.

20 OCT Smith and Wright both score to secure a crucial 2–1 first-leg win at Danish club Brondby.

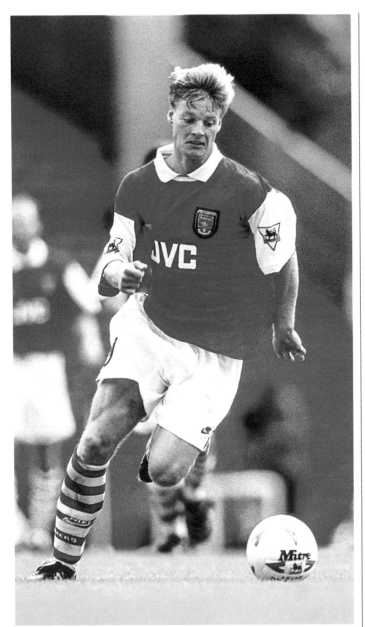

New signing Stefan Schwarz made an immediate impact after his £1.75 million move from Benfica

23 OCT A mixed day for Ian Wright: he scores in his tenth consecutive game for Arsenal, breaking David Jack's 63-year-old record, but his seventh booking of the season earns him a three-match ban and he picks up a groin injury.

25 NOV Paul Merson shocks the footballing world by admitting his addiction to drink, drugs and gambling. Both the FA and the club offer him total support.

30 NOV Steve Morrow scores his second goal for the Gunners – again against Sheffield Wednesday, this time in a 2–0 victory in the Coca-Cola Cup fourth round.

1 DEC Merson escapes punishment by the FA, but must undergo a four- to six-week rehabilitation programme.

2 DEC The Premier League confirms Wright's goal

against Newcastle in September, giving him a new club record: he has scored in 12 consecutive League and Cup games. Meanwhile Tony Adams is ruled out for two months after an Achilles operation.

1 DEC Graham repays £425,000 to the club.

4 DEC The *Mail on Sunday* reveals that Graham accepted a secret payment of £285,000 from a Norwegian agent in the transfer of John Jensen in 1992.

15 DEC The Premier League sets up a three-man commission to inquire into the allegations against Graham.

18 DEC It emerges that Graham has admitted to the commission that he has returned more than £400,000 to Arsenal, not just the £285,000 from the Jensen deal.

19 DEC Graham receives the support of the Arsenal board, even though commission member Steve Coppell declares: "It's clear and obvious George Graham took the money."

31 DEC Another shock for the incredulous Arsenal fans: John Jensen scores. QPR still win 3–1, though, despite a spectacular strike from the Danish midfielder.

7 JAN Millwall hold Arsenal to a 0–0 draw at the New Den in the FA Cup third round, a day after Ian Wright accuses the Millwall fans of racism.

11 JAN Liverpool's Ian Rush scores the only goal to deny Arsenal a place in the Coca-Cola Cup semi-finals.

13 JAN George Graham suddenly decides to splash out, making Luton striker John Hartson England's

Paul Merson left his lager-lager goal celebration behind when he faced up to his drink problem

most expensive teenager at £2.5 million while also signing Chris Kiwomya from struggling Ipswich Town (the tribunal later sets the price at £1.25 million). The Premier League commission spends three hours interviewing Norwegian agent Rune Hauge.

18 JAN Millwall dump Arsenal out of the FA Cup at the third round stage, winning 2–0 in the replay at Highbury.

22 JAN New revelations in the *Mail on Sunday* allege that Graham also received £145,000 from the deal which brought Pal Lydersen to Highbury in November 1991.

30 JAN Wright is banned for four matches and fined a record £1,000 after accumulating 41 penalty points.

1 FEB Paul Merson returns to action, coming on for the last 15 minutes of the 0–0 draw with Milan in the European Super Cup first leg.

4 FEB Both Tony Adams and John Hartson are sent off in a 3–1 defeat by Sheffield Wednesday.

8 FEB Milan win 2–0 in the European Super Cup return leg.

14 FEB Dutch winger Glenn Helder arrives from Vitesse Arnhem for £2 million.

17 FEB The Premier League shows its report both to the Arsenal board and to Graham himself.

20 FEB Reports emerge that the commission has found Graham guilty of taking a "bung" and the Arsenal board decides to sack the manager.

21 FEB Graham is dimissed for failing "to act in the best interests of the club". In his first game in charge, caretaker-manager Stewart Houston sees the Gunners achieve their first League win at Highbury in four months, in a 1–0 victory over Forest.

23 FEB The Premier League chief executive confirms that Graham has been found guilty of receiving £425,500 from Hauge and has returned this sum, plus £40,000 interest, to the club.

1 MAR Auxerre hold the Gunners to a 1–1 draw at Highbury in the first leg of their Cup-Winners' Cup quarter-final.

16 MAR In the return match in France, Wright hits a spectacular first-half goal to book a semi-final place.

6 APR Arsenal threaten to squander a 2–0 lead in the first leg of their semi-final with Sampdoria, but they finish the game 3–2 winners, Ian Wright scoring the third after earlier goals by Steve Bould.

20 APR David Seaman again performs heroics in a shoot-out, saving shots from three Sampdoria players after Arsenal had lost the second leg 3–2: a late goal from Stefan Schwarz had kept the Gunners in the competition, setting up a second successive year in the Cup-Winners' Cup final.

10 MAY Former Tottenham player Nayim scores an improbable winner in the very last minute of extra

 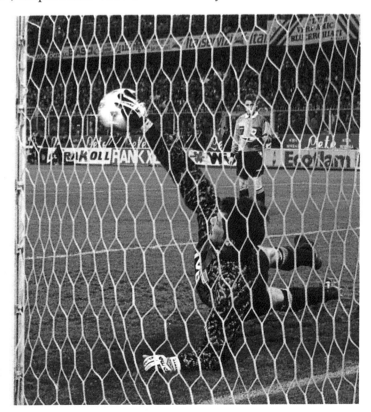

David Seaman's third shoot-out save against Sampdoria sends Arsenal to the Cup-Winners' Cup final

time to wrest the Cup-Winners' Cup from Arsenal's grip in the cruellest manner. John Hartson had earlier scored Arsenal's equalizer, to take the game into extra time.

17 MAY The unfortunate David Seaman receives another setback, breaking an ankle on Arsenal's Far Eastern tour.

30 MAY Former Arsenal and England centre-forward Ted Drake dies at the age of 82.

6 JUNE Bobby Robson declines an offer to take over at Highbury, deciding to remain with Porto.

8 JUNE Bruce Rioch, having just taken Bolton into the Premiership, takes over as the new Arsenal manager.

20 JUNE Dutch striker Dennis Bergkamp becomes Rioch's first signing, and Arsenal's most expensive player, joining from Inter for £7.5 million.

30 JUNE Kevin Campbell, no doubt taking heed of Bergkamp's arrival, decides to join Nottingham Forest in a £2.8 million deal.

1995–96

10 JULY Rioch pulls off another coup, bringing England captain David Platt back from Italy: Sampdoria demand £4.75 million for the midfielder.

12 JULY George Graham is found guilty of taking illegal payments from Rune Hauge's Interclub Ltd. as part of the Lydersen and Jensen transfers.

13 JULY Graham is banned from football for a year.

14 JULY Stefan Schwarz is granted a transfer after one season in England, joining Fiorentina for £2 million.

19 JULY Alan Smith, who joined the club from Leicester in 1987, announces his retirement due to a knee injury.

26 JULY Dennis Bergkamp takes just six minutes to score his first Arsenal hat-trick as the side romps to an 8–1 win over Swedish side Kristianstads.

23 SEPT Bergkamp scores his first League goals in an Arsenal shirt, netting twice in a 4–2 win over Southampton.

10 OCT Steve Bould wins his first England cap, lining up alongside Adams in the goalless draw in Norway.

28 OCT The club complains to the FA, alleging that Wright was subjected to racist abuse by Barnsley fans and stewards at their Coca-Cola Cup game at Oakwell.

9 NOV Arsenal beat Sampdoria 2–0 at Highbury in Alan Smith's testimonial.

29 NOV Ian Wright's 250th goal propels the Gunners into the Coca-Cola Cup quarter-finals in a 2–1 win over Sheffield Wednesday.

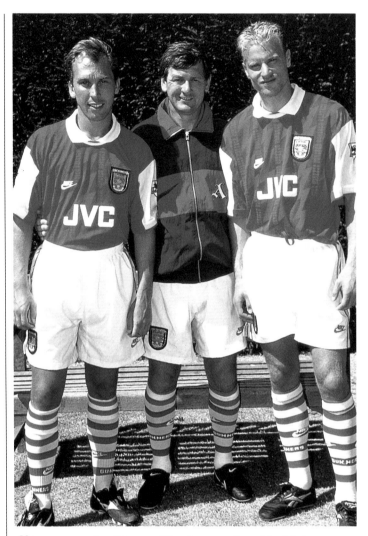

New manager Bruce Rioch parades his big-money signings, David Platt and Dennis Bergkamp

6 JAN Sheffield United leave Highbury with a 1–1 draw in the third round of the FA Cup.

10 JAN Ian Wright scores twice to knock Newcastle out of the Coca-Cola Cup at the quarter-final stage, with United winger David Ginola sent off, prompting a touchline clash between the two benches.

12 JAN Manchester United are found guilty of poaching 16-year-old defender Matthew Wicks from the Gunners.

17 JAN Carl Veart's goal for Sheffield United sends Arsenal tumbling out of the FA Cup in a third-round replay.

7 FEB Arsenal are represented at a UEFA summit in Geneva, which recommends an expansion of European club competitions, as part of which England and another seven countries would each enter two sides in the Champions' League.

10 FEB Bergkamp scores the only goal to end Nottingham Forest's 26-match unbeaten run at home.

Rioch takes on the Newcastle bench after David Ginola's sending off. Arsenal win the quarter-final 2–0

13 FEB Rioch is warned by the FA for his involvement in the touchline fracas with Newcastle assistant manager Terry McDermott at the Coca-Cola Cup quarter-final in January.

14 FEB Bergkamp scores twice, but Arsenal concede two crucial away goals to Aston Villa in the first leg of their Coca-Cola Cup semi-final at Highbury.

21 FEB Villa hold out for a goalless draw in the return leg, denying the Gunners a place in the final.

1 MAR The club renews its sponsorship deal with JVC for another three years.

12 MAR Cult hero John Jensen returns to Danish side Brondby on loan for the remainder of the season.

13 MAR The Arsenal board reject a transfer request from the disgruntled Ian Wright.

23 MAR Scott Marshall and Ian Wright score the goals which threaten to derail Newcastle's Championship challenge.

5 MAY Late goals from Platt and Bergkamp on the final day of the season defeat Rioch's former club Bolton 2–1, and book the Gunners a place in next season's UEFA Cup.

1996–97

12 AUG Bruce Rioch is sensationally sacked just five days before the new season starts, his only summer signing having brought John Lukic back from Leeds. Stewart Houston is again appointed caretaker-manager.

20 AUG Speculation that Arsène Wenger, manager of Japanese side Grampus Eight, is being lined up to take over are fuelled by the arrival of two new French signings, Patrick Vieira from Milan and Remi Garde from Strasbourg.

13 SEPT Highbury is plunged into more uncertainty when Houston resigns, deciding to take charge at London neighbours QPR. Pat Rice becomes the Gunners' second caretaker boss in a month.

15 SEPT Skipper Tony Adams admits he has been receiving treatment for alcoholism. The following day, Wenger affirms his support for the Arsenal captain.

7 SEPT Late goals from Paul Merson and Andy Linighan snatch a 2–2 draw at Aston Villa.

10 SEPT Wright and Merson both score, but Arsenal lose 3–2 at home in the first leg of their opening UEFA Cup game with Borussia Mönchengladbach.

16 SEPT Vieira makes his Arsenal debut in the 4–1 win over League leaders Sheffield Wednesday, an Ian Wright hat-trick completing his century of League goals for the club.

25 SEPT Both Wright and Merson get on the scoresheet again, but Mönchengladbach again score three, putting an end to Arsenal's European campaign at the first hurdle.

28 SEPT Wenger finally arrives in England, and is formally announced as new Arsenal manager, meaning Rice goes down as the only Highbury boss to enjoy a 100% success-rate while in charge.

15 OCT The FA charges Wright with misconduct over comments made about Sheffield Wednesday manager David Pleat.

26 OCT George Graham makes an unhappy return to Highbury, Arsenal beating his new Leeds side 3–0; all three goals are scored in the opening 10 minutes.

1 NOV Controversial trio Adams, Wright and Merson are all recalled to the England squad for the World Cup qualifier against Georgia.

16 NOV Nigel Winterburn scores an own goal for Manchester United in a 1–0 defeat at Old Trafford. Wright clashes with United goalkeeper Peter Schmeichel, and later accuses the Danish international of racist abuse.

24 NOV Wenger's first North London derby ends in dramatic fashion, with spectacular goals from Tony Adams and Dennis Bergkamp in the last few minutes securing a thrilling 3–1 triumph for the Gunners.

27 NOV Liverpool win the Coca-Cola Cup fourth round tie at Anfield, despite two goals from Ian Wright; Steve Bould is sent off in a 4–2 defeat.

30 NOV Tony Adams is controversially sent off after a clash with Newcastle and England striker Alan Shearer at St. James's Park, but Arsenal defy the League leaders' pressure, and come away with a hard-won 2–1 victory: Ian Wright scores the winning goal.

7 DEC Vieira scores his first goal for the club, a last-minute equalizer, to salvage a 2–2 draw with Derby County.

21 DEC Ian Wright is sent off after an off-the-ball altercation with Nottingham Forest's Nicola Jerkan, and the Gunners slip to a 2–1 defeat in Stuart Pearce's first game in charge at the City Ground.

28 DEC The Gunners again leave it late against Villa, but again achieve a 2–2 draw, with goals from Wright and Merson.

31 DEC David Seaman is awarded an MBE in the New Year's Honours List, at the end of the year in which he starred in Euro 96.

11 JAN Adams scores a bizarre own goal and Bergkamp is shown the red card as the Gunners lose 1–0 at struggling Sunderland.

22 JAN Andy Linighan, goalscoring hero of the 1992 FA Cup Final, moves to First Division Crystal Palace on a free transfer.

4 FEB George Graham puts one over his old club in the FA Cup fourth round at Elland Road: a Rod Wallace goal is enough to knock Arsenal out of the competition.

7 FEB John Hartson moves across London to West Ham United, in a deal worth around £4 million. He still manages to raise a smile at Highbury by scoring in his first game for the Hammers – a 4–3 defeat of Tottenham.

15 FEB Lukic, again deputizing for the injured Seaman, makes a string of crucial saves in the 0–0 draw at Tottenham.

19 FEB Arsenal again waste an opportunity to go top, losing 2–1 at home to Manchester United. Wright and Schmeichel again confront each other, both during and after the game.

23 FEB Wenger moves swiftly to poach French starlet Nicolas Anelka from Paris St. Germain, who had only signed apprentice terms with the French club.

Patrick Vieira's classy last-minute goal salvages a 2–2 draw with Derby

seems to disagree – and record a 2–1 victory in the crucial Championship clash.

5 APR In a Saturday-morning fixture Arsenal run out comfortable 3–0 winners away to London neighbours Chelsea, with Anelka making his debut as an 85th-minute substitute.

6 APR Manchester United manager Alex Ferguson takes Wenger to task after the Arsenal boss advises the FA not to allow United more time to complete their season. Ferguson rages: "He doesn't know anything about English football and the demands of our game."

14 APR Ian Wright picks up third place at the PFA Player of the Year awards ceremony, behind winner Alan Shearer and youthful runner-up David Beckham.

10 MAY Luton's 18-year-old defender Matthew Upson joins Arsenal for a fee of £2 million.

11 MAY Tony Adams is sent off for the second time this season, but Arsenal come from behind to beat Derby 3–1 and finish the season in third place – good enough to qualify for the 1997–98 UEFA Cup.

2 JUNE Inter's Paul Ince attacks Blackburn and Arsenal, both of whom are thought to consider him too old to be worth a high transfer fee.

4 JUNE Wenger raids his old club Monaco to bring French stars Gilles Grimandi and Emmanuel Petit to Highbury.

17 JUNE Marc Overmars joins Dutch compatriot Dennis Bergkamp at the Gunners for £7 million from Ajax, along with Portugese striker Luis Boamorte and German midfielder Alberto Mendez-Rodriguez.

7 JULY Paul Merson makes a shock departure from the club, dropping down a division to join Middlesbrough for £5 million.

15 MAR A triumph for the Arsenal youngsters, as the promising Paul Shaw and Stephen Hughes both score in the 2–0 win at Southampton.

18 MAR Austrian goalkeeper Alex Manninger impresses on his trial at the club, and becomes Wenger's latest signing.

20 MAR Martin Keown returns to the international scene, named in England's squad for the friendly with Mexico.

24 MAR Liverpool are awarded a controversial penalty at Highbury – with which even Robbie Fowler

Ireland's Glentoran. Goals from Graham (two) and future Wales manager Bobby Gould brought Highbury its first sight of a victorious Arsenal in European competition. Arsenal went on to win 3–1 on aggregate, dispose of Sporting Club of Lisbon 3–0 overall in the second round, Rouen of France by 1–0 in the third round and Dinamo Bacau of Romania 9–1 to reach the semi-finals and a duel with Holland's Ajax Amsterdam.

The previous season Ajax had finished runners-up in the senior Champions' Cup. Their prodigious, slim-line centre-forward Johan Cruyff was attracting rave notices everywhere he appeared. His day against Arsenal would come – but not yet. Two goals in the last 13 minutes of the first leg from George and Sammels earned a 3–0 win at Highbury. Arsenal conceded an early strike to Gerrie Muhren in Amsterdam, but their increasingly fearsome defence held tight for the rest of the 90 minutes.

Arsenal were comparative late-comers in the pursuit of European glory. Seven other Football League clubs had already enjoyed the thrill of appearing in Continental cup finals – Manchester United (1968) in the Champions' Cup; Tottenham (1963), West Ham (1965) and Liverpool (1966) in the Cup-Winners' Cup; and then Birmingham City (1960 and 1961), Leeds United (1967 and 1968) and Newcastle United (1969) in the Fairs Cup.

Anderlecht of Brussels were the neutrals' favourites. They had been competing in Europe since the mid-1950s and had, for much of the 1960s, provided the backbone of an excellent Belgian national team. Forward Paul Van Himst would ultimately be hailed as the greatest Belgian player of all time.

The first leg went according to the neutrals' plan. Dutchmen Jan Devrindt and Jan Mulder (twice) shot their Belgian employers into a 3–0 lead by the 76th minute. Then Mee gambled by introducing the young tyro, Ray Kennedy, as substitute for the tiring Graham. Within five minutes he had pulled one goal back – and a crucial goal it proved.

A 52,000-strong crowd filled Highbury to bursting

Semi-final success: Jon Sammels scores the second in the 1970 Fairs semi-final first leg against Ajax

point for the return. Eddie Kelly, tireless in attack and defence, cracked the opening goal after 25 minutes. Radford scored a second and Sammels the aggregate winner, in the 71st minute.

Arsenal, uncrowned kings of Europe under Chapman in the 1930s, had at last claimed an international trophy – 40 years on. More than that, they had forged the team spirit and confidence which would lift them, a year later, to win the prized English double of League and FA Cup.

The Seventies

Inter Cities Fairs Cup 1970–71

The pressure of a domestic fixture pile-up proved fatal to Arsenal's hopes of retaining the Fairs Cup. After overcoming Lazio – whose players set upon Arsenal's stars after the match – Sturm Graz and Beveren Waas, they fell to Germany's Cologne on the away goals rule in the quarter-finals.

But who cared? Arsenal soon had bigger fish to fry as their 1971 league title earned promotion, for the first time, into the Champions Cup, most prestigious international club event in the world.

European Cup 1971–72

Mee believed that Arsenal could win the Cup. They had a solid defence, an opportunist attack and plenty of big-match experience both at home and abroad. Stromgodset of Norway were despatched 7–1 on aggregate and Grasshopper Zurich 5–0 overall. But then, in the quarter-finals, the fabled luck of the Arsenal deserted them for once – the Gunners found themselves paired with European champions Ajax.

This was not the naïve, easily–depressed Ajax whom Arsenal had beaten in the 1970 Fairs semi-final. This was an Ajax side justly acknowledged as the best in the world. Their "total football" had taken Europe by storm. Arsenal were disappointed, at the time, to lose 2–1 away and 1–0 at home. But with the perspective of time, the truth of the matter is that they did well to give Cruyff and Co. such a close run for their guilders over the 180 minutes of the tie.

Arsenal opened the scoring in the first leg, in Amsterdam, when Kennedy pounced on a defensive

Bitter end: Valencia keeper Pereira saves Graham Rix's kick in the 1980 Cup-winners' Cup Final

slip at a free-kick. But unlucky Peter Simpson deflected a Muhren shot past Wilson for the equalizer and a controversial late penalty provided Ajax with their winner. Mee had strengthened his team, domestically, by signing World Cup-winning midfielder Alan Ball, but he was ineligible for Europe and, for the return leg at Highbury, they were also deprived of Radford through suspension. George Graham scored the only goal … in his own net.

UEFA Cup 1978–79
Arsenal were thus eliminated not merely from the Champions' Cup but from all European competition for more than six years. In 1978–79 they returned, in the Fairs Cup, only to fall to Red Star Belgrade in the third round. But memory of that defeat was left behind a few months later by the FA Cup success which promoted them into the Cup-Winners' Cup for the first time in 1979–80.

Cup-Winners' Cup 1979–80

Now under the managerial guidance of Terry Neill, Arsenal had rebuilt their dreams around a nucleus of outstanding discoveries including Irish midfielder Liam Brady. Fenerbahce of Turkey were the first-round opposition. Arsenal coach Don Howe had worked in Turkey for their rivals, Galatasaray, and was under no illusions about the task in hand. Goals from Alan Sunderland and Willie Young brought a 2–0 win at Highbury, while a goalless draw in Istanbul earned a second-round meeting against the inhospitable East Germans of Magdeburg.

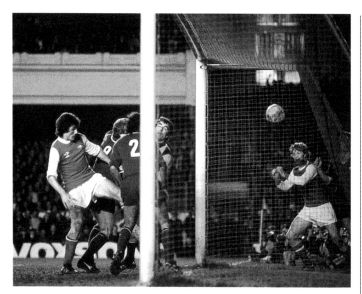

Scrambled: Juventus's Roberto Bettega puts though his own goal – for Arsenal at Highbury

Five years earlier Magdeburg had surprised Europe by winning the Cup-Winners' Cup: the German Democratic Republic's only European club trophy. But by now, the edge had gone off the team. Arsenal won only 2–1 at home but defied East German over-confidence to secure a 2–2 draw beyond "the Wall".

The beauty of the Cup-Winners' Cup – compared with the UEFA Cup – is that two aggregate victories lift a club into the quarter-finals. Here Arsenal gained a bonus by being drawn against the Swedes of IFK Gothenburg. The Angels of Gothenburg were not quite yet the outstanding side who would later upset a lot of form favourites in the Champions' League. They were also rusty after their winter break and crashed 5–1 at Highbury. Arsenal might easily have won even more convincingly, and strolled confidently to a 0–0 draw in Sweden.

So far, so good. Arsenal had played six games, won three, drawn three and lost none. But Juventus in the semi-finals were a far tougher test – literally. They even took the lead at Highbury and, though midfielder Marco Tardelli was sent off and Roberto Bettega put through his own goal, held out for a 1–1 draw.

The return could not have come at a more challenging time for the Gunners, who went to Turin in the middle of an FA Cup semi-final saga with Liverpool. Remarkably, they won 1–0 with a goal from youngster Paul Vaessen, who was then unknown to most English fans, let alone the Italians.

That was Arsenal's last celebration of the season. Liverpool left them trailing in the League, they lost 1–0 to West Ham United in the FA Cup Final … and, four days later, fell to Valencia of Spain in the final of the Cup-Winners' Cup.

The Heysel stadium in Brussels, scene five years later of the most horrific events at any European final, was the venue. Valencia boasted Mario Kempes, Argentina's World Cup-winning inspiration from 1978 – not that he ever threatened Arsenal. David O'Leary covered his every stride across the penalty box. After a stifling, defence-dominated, fear-ridden match, Kempes failed even in the penalty shoot-out. But so did Brady – being watched by both Barcelona and Juventus – and so, disastrously, did Graham Rix. Valencia thus claimed the Cup 5–4 on penalties.

The Eighties

UEFA Cup 1981–82 / 1982–83

The 1980s were a period of triumph and trauma for English football in Europe. A matter of weeks after Arsenal lost to Valencia, England's national team were shamed by the antics of a minority of hooligans at the European Championship finals in Turin. While the Champions' Cup was carried home by Liverpool, Aston Villa and then Liverpool again, and results on the pitch were as good as ever, the hooligans spread an ever-increasing trail of destruction across the Continent.

Arsenal, ironically, were spared any association with the growing storm by their own failures. They qualified for the UEFA Cup in 1981–82, but crashed in the second round to Winterslag of Belgium, and fell in 1982–83, in the first round, to Moscow Spartak.

Two years later events at Heysel, where Arsenal had fallen to Valencia, led to the expulsion of all English clubs from European competition for five long years.

The Nineties

Champions' Cup 1991–92

In Arsenal's case, absence from Europe lasted nine years between their UEFA Cup defeat by Spartak in the autumn of 1982 and their return, in the

Champions' Cup, in the autumn of 1991. The Gunners – thanks to the Chapman legacy – have always harboured grand notions of a place among the aristocracy of European club football. But the Champions' Cup, most prestigious proving-ground for the ambitious, has yet to see the best of Arsenal. They were unable to enter in 1989–90 because of the English ban and paid for their European inexperience in 1991–92.

FK Austria were crushed in the first round. Arsenal won 6–1 at home with four goals from Alan Smith, and the subsequent 1–0 defeat in Vienna mattered not at all. With hindsight, the margin of success was deceptive. The rest of Europe in general – and second round rivals Benfica in particular – were not prepared to be such instant fall guys.

The rewards for the winners were immense – a place in the lucrative mini-league section which, that season, straddled the middle of the European fixture calendar. Arsenal thought they had achieved the hardest part when they forced a 1–1 draw in the first leg in the Stadium of Light: Kevin Campbell hit back within five minutes of Isaias having opened the score for Benfica.

Two weeks later, the return appeared a formality. But Arsenal and English football had a sharp lesson to learn. While England's clubs had been out of Europe, the Europeans – always superior in terms of technique – had caught up in terms of fitness and physical preparation. Back at Highbury, Benfica matched Arsenal physically through the regulation 90 minutes and into extra-time, where their superior technique won the day.

Central defender Colin Pates opened the scoring after 20 minutes only for Isaias to equalize a quarter of an hour later. Soviet international sweeper Vasili Kulkov stifled Arsenal's hopes 11 minutes into extra-time. The Gunners now needed to score twice to overcome Benfica's away-goals advantage. Their desperation left gaps at the back which Isaias exploited to score a third for the Portuguese champions.

Such failure was particularly galling for manager George Graham since he had known the European glory days with Arsenal as a player and was fascinated by all

All ours! Arsenal triumph in the 1994 Cup-Winners' Cup, watched by UEFA president Lennart Johansson

The winner: Alan Smith shoots Arsenal ahead against Parma in Copenhagen

things Continental – the technical preparation, the dietary controls and the tactical disciplines.

Cup-Winners' Cup 1993–94

The lessons Graham had learned were put into practice with the greatest success in the Cup-Winners' Cup in 1993–94. Arsenal ultimately carried off the Cup – belated reward after their narrow failure in 1980 – and earned extra credit for doing so in a season when the secondary competition carried more glamour than the Champions' Cup itself.

Apart from Arsenal, with their legendary name, the challengers to Italian holders Parma included Real Madrid, Ajax Amsterdam, Benfica and the rising French power, Paris Saint-Germain.

Odense of Denmark were no problem in the first round. Arsenal won 3–2 on aggregate before sensationally thrashing Belgium's Standard Liège 10–0 overall in the second round. Two goals from Ian Wright inspired a 3–0 success at home which pro-

voked all sorts of internal problems at Liège. The Belgians were in no mood for the second leg and even their own fans ended up cheering Arsenal, who scorched to a 7–0 success in the Sclessin stadium.

Arsenal had not progressed beyond the quarter-finals in a European competition since the 1980 Cup-Winners' Cup. Graham was determined that this time there would be no slip-ups. Accordingly, he plotted the tactical battle with Torino in the quarters down to the last detail. The first leg, in Turin, ended 0–0. The second, at Highbury, was decided by a 65th-minute goal from skipper Tony Adams, heading home a Paul Davis free-kick.

The semi-finals matched Arsenal against Paris S-G. The French, having defeated Real Madrid with some panache in the quarter-finals, were the neutrals' favourites. They had gone 35 matches without defeat, were virtually certain of winning the French league and could indulge their own European fantasies.

Not for much longer. In the 35th minute, another penetrating Davis free-kick split Paris' off-side trap, and this time Wright was in place to score. The French equalized through David Ginola early in the second half, but now the balance in the tie had altered. Campbell headed home after only seven minutes of the second half, and Arsenal exerted a vice-like grip on the rest of the match to secure their tickets to Copenhagen for the final.

No club, in the history of the Cup-Winners' Cup, have ever retained the trophy for a second successive season. Parma believed they could break the jinx, and might have done so had Sweden's Tomas Brolin taken advantage of two gilt-edged opportunities in only the first 15 minutes of the final in the Parkstadion.

Four more minutes and Arsenal were in charge. Parma skipper Lorenzo Minotti miscued a clearance attempt and Alan Smith, hardly believing his luck, strode forward and unleashed a left-foot shot which clipped the inside of the near post and ricocheted into the far corner to give the Gunners the lead.

Cup-Winners' Cup 1994–95

This was, to all intents and purposes, the long-awaited springboard towards a place in the European superleague to which Arsenal aspired. Progress off the pitch, under the eagle eye of vice-chairman David Dein, saw the redevelopment of Highbury stadium underpinned by an aggressive commercial and promotional policy.

But football has an odd habit of upsetting the best-laid plans, and Arsenal's defence of the Cup-Winners' Cup proved the point. Just like Parma the previous season, they found their way back to the final. Then, again just like Parma had done, they let it slip through their fingers by the narrowest of margins.

Ironically, that season's Cup-Winners' Cup did not contain anything like the same quality of potential opposition. Ian Wright was the individual star. He scored three goals in the 6–1 defeat of Omonia of Cyprus in the first round and two more in the 4–3 elimination of Denmark's Brondby in the second. Wright scored the goals, both home and away, with which Arsenal overcame Auxerre of France 2–1 on aggregate in the quarter-finals. He then scored in each leg of the semi-final against Sampdoria – before England goalkeeper David Seaman took on the hero's mantle with his penalty saves.

Arsenal beat Sampdoria 3–2 at home and lost 3–2 away. That meant the Gunners' first penalty shoot-out since the painful failure against Valencia in 1980. Now

All square: John Hartson equalizes against Zaragoza in the 1995 Cup-winners' Cup Final

it was their turn to enjoy fortune's smile. Seaman saved the kicks of Sinisa Mihajlovic, Vladimir Jugovic and Attilio Lombardo and the Gunners had made it, by a 3–2 shoot-out margin.

But David Seaman's unhappy "reward" for his semi-final heroics was to be cast as the scapegoat in the final. Playing against the under-rated Spanish side Real

Paris agony: Nayim's last-second lob drops behind David Seaman's fingers

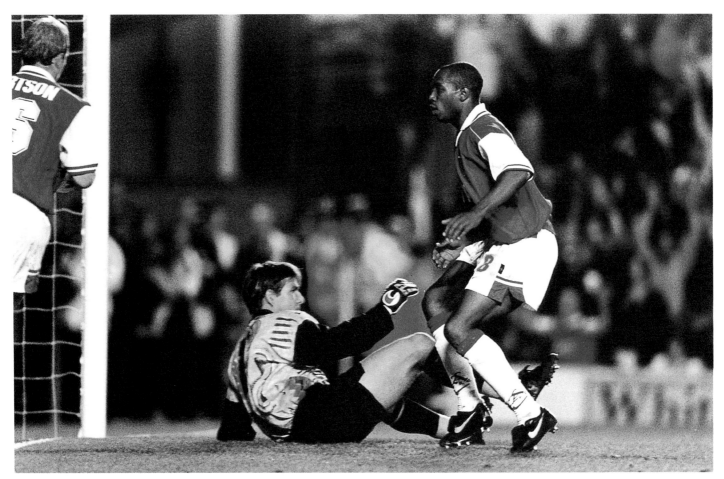

Ian Wright scores – too late – against Borussia Mönchengladbach at Highbury in the 1996–97 UEFA Cup

Zaragoza in the Parc des Princes in Paris.

A tight match saw Zaragoza snatch the lead with a superb strike-on-the-turn by Argentine forward Juan Esnaider midway through the second half. Arsenal needed a touch of Ian Wright's magic but, for the first time in the competition, he found the way to goal blocked and it was left to the young Welshman, John Hartson, to score the equalizer which earned extra-time.

As the match drew on, closer loomed the prospect of a penalty shoot-out in which Arsenal, with Seaman to fill the goalmouth, would be favourites.

But, with Italian referee Ceccarini looking at his watch, Zaragoza struck the fantastic, decisive blow. Midfielder Nayim, way out on the right, hit a towering lob high in the direction of goal. The lights in the Parc des Princes are hung from the roof of the stand and Seaman, looking up into the lights as he ran back, lost the trajectory of the ball … which fell behind him, just under the bar, and into the net.

It was a fearsomely dramatic way in which to lose a match – let alone a cup. Even worse, of course, Nayim himself had only recently returned to Spain after a spell with Arsenal's rivals, the Premiership's other north Londoners, Tottenham Hotspur.

The price of defeat was a heavy one. Arsenal had struggled in the League. Retaining the Cup-Winners' Cup had been their last vain hope of a return to European competition in 1995–96.

UEFA Cup 1996–97

A return to European duty some 18 months later in the 1996–97 UEFA Cup ended all too soon at the hands of Borussia Mönchengladbach in the first-round. Arsenal were behind 3–1 in the first-leg at Highbury when Ian Wright gave the team a life-line for the second leg with a last-minute goal. But an identical scoreline – with Ian Wright and Paul Merson once again providing Arsenal's strikes – saw the club crash out of the competition 6–4 on aggregate.

Despite all the pioneering work of the inter-war years, despite success in the Fairs Cup and the Cup-Winners' Cup, a gap remains in the trophy cabinet. The biggest prize of all, the Champions' Cup, is still out there, waiting.

Arsenal in Europe-The Complete Record

First Round	Second Round	Third Round	Quarter-Final	Semi-Final	Final
1961-62 - Inter - City Fairs Record					
vs Staevnet (Denmark) (a) W 7–1 (Radford 2,George 2, Sammels 2, Graham) (h) L 2–3 (Skirton, Barnwell)	vs FC Liège (Belgium) (h) D 1–1 (T Anderson) (a) L 1–3 (McCullough)				
1969-70 - Inter - City Fairs Cup					
vs Glentoran (N Ireland) (h) W 3–0 (Graham 2, Gould) (a) L 0–1	vs Sporting Lisbon (Portugal) (a) D 0–0 (h) W 3–0 (Radford, Graham 2)	vs Rouen (France) (a) D 0–0 (h) W 1–0 (Sammels)	vs Dinamo Bacau (Romania) (a) W 2–0 (Sammels, Radford) (h) W 7–1 (Radford 2, George 2, Graham, Sammels 2)	vs Ajax Amsterdam (Holland) (h) W 3–0 (George 2, 1 pen, Sammels) (a) L 0–1	vs Anderlecht (Belgium) (a) L 1–3 (Kennedy) (h) W 3–0 (Kelly, Radford, Sammels)
1970–71 – Inter-City Fairs Cup					
vs Lazio (Italy) (a) D 2–2 (Radford 2) (h) W 2–0 (Radford, Armstrong)	Sturm Graz (Austria) (a) L 0–1 (h) W 2–0 (Kennedy, Storey pen)	vs Beveren Waas (Belgium) (h) W 4–0 (Graham, Sammels, Kennedy 2) (a) D 0–0	vs Cologne (W Germany) (h) W 2–1 (McLintock, Storey) (a) L 0–1		
1971–72 – Champions' Cup					
vs Stromgodset (Norway) (a) W 3–1 (Simpson, Walker, og) (h) W 3–0 (Kennedy, Radford 2, Armstrong)	vs Grasshoppers (Switzerland) (a) W 2–0 (Kennedy, Graham) (h) W 3–0 (Kennedy, George, Radford)		Ajax Amsterdam (Holland) (a) L 1–2 (Kennedy) (h) L 0–1		
1978–79 – UEFA Cup					
vs Lokomotive Leipzig (E Germany) (h) W 3–0 (Stapleton 2, Sunderland) (a) W 4–1 (Brady, Stapleton 2, Sunderland)	vs Hajduk Split (Yugoslavia) (a) L 1–2 (Brady) (h) W 1–0 (Young)	vs Red Star Belgrade (Yugoslavia) (a) L 0–1 (h) L 1–1 (Sunderland)			
1979–80 – Cup-winners' Cup					
vs Fenerbahce (Turkey)) (h) W 2–0 (Sunderland, Young) (a) D 0–0	vs Magdeburg (E Germany) (h) W 2–1 (Young, Sunderland) (a) D 2–2 (Price, Brady)		vs IFK Gothenburg (Sweden) (h) W 5–0 (Sunderland 2, Price, Brady, Young) (a) D 0–0	vs Juventus (Italy) (h) D 1–1 (Bettega og) (a) W 1–0 (Vaessen)	vs Valencia (Spain) at Brussels D 0–0 (L 4–5 pens)
1981–82 – UEFA Cup					
vs Panathinaikos (Greece) (a) W 2–0 (McDermott, Meade) (h) W 1–0 (Talbot)	vs Winterslag (Belgium) (a) L 0–1 (h) W 2–1 (Hollins, Rix)				
1982–83 – UEFA Cup					
vs Moscow Spartak (USSR) (a) L 2–3 (Robson, Chapman) (h) L 2–5 (McDermott, Chapman)					
1991–92 – Champions' Cup					
vs FK Austria (Austria)) (h) W 6–1 (Smith 4, Linighan, Limpar) (a) L 0–1	Benfica (Portugal) (a) D 1–1 (Campbell) (h) L 1–3 (Pates)				
1993–94 – Cup-winners' Cup					
vs Odense (Denmark) (a) W 2–1 (Wright, Merson) (h) D 1–1 (Campbell)	vs Standard Liège (Belgium) (h) W 3–0 (Wright 2, Merson) (a) W 7–0 (Smith, Selley, Adams, Campbell 2, Merson, McGoldrick)		vs Torino (Italy) (a) D 0–0 (h) W 1–0 (Adams)	vs Paris St Germain (France) (a) D 1–1 (Wright) (h) W 1–0 (Campbell)	vs Parma (Italy) at Copenhagen W 1–0 (Smith)
1994–95 – Cup-winners' Cup					
vs Omonia (Cyprus) (a) W 3–1 (Merson 2, Wright) (h) W 3–0 (Wright 2, Schwartz)	vs Brondy (Denmark) (a) W 2–1 (Wright, Smith) (h) D 2–2 (Wright pen, Selley)		vs Auxerre (France) (h) D 1–1 (Wright pen) (a) W 1–0 (Wright)	vs Sampdoria (Italy) (h) W 3–2(Bould 2, Wright) (a) L 2–3 (aet) (Wright, Schwartz) W 3–2 on pens	Real Zaragoza (Spain) at Paris L 1–2 (aet) (Hartson)
1996–97 – UEFA Cup					
vs Borussia Mönchengladbach (Germany) (h) L 2–3 (Wright, Merson) (a) L 2–3 (Wright, Merson)					

Chapter 4

Up for the Cup

Arsenal's reputation has been founded on the strength of character which is rewarded by consistent success in league championship campaigns. Yet the Gunners' history has also been packed with drama

Arsenal's relationship with the two domestic cups has been characterized by peaks and troughs.

The Highbury history books record such triumphs as the FA Cup win that clinched the double in 1970–71, the "Five-Minute Final" of 1978–79 and the unique double-Cup success of 1992–93: but equally noteworthy are the ignominious Cup humiliations, ranging from Walsall in the 1930s and then York, Oxford and Walsall again in the 1980s to Wrexham, Bolton and Millwall in the 1990s.

But while North London neighbours Tottenham are more famously known as a "Cup-winning side", Arsenal possess an equally impressive pedigree in the knock-out competitions. In six FA Cup triumphs and two League Cup successes – not to mention the eight times an Arsenal captain has got his hands on the FA Charity Shield – Arsenal's red-and-white colours have been ribboned to silverware throughout the club's history.

Early successes

Within just a few years of the club's birth, Arsenal were tasting Cup triumph. In the 1889–90 season the side picked up the London Charity Cup, as well as the Kent Senior Cup and the Kent Junior Cup, going on to win the London Senior Cup the following season by thumping St. Bartholomew's Hospital 6–0 at the Oval.

It was not until the 1900–01 season that Arsenal first reached beyond the first round proper of the FA Cup, beating Blackburn 2–0 but losing 1–0 to West Bromwich Albion in the second round. Within a couple of seasons, however, the club were making considerable strides. The 1905–06 campaign saw Arsenal, under the tutelage of Phil Kelso, not only get through the second round for the first time in the club's history but reach the semi-finals, despatching the mighty Sunderland and Manchester United en route.

If Arsenal's progress that year was a surprise, it was even greater the following season when they again reached the semi-finals, falling to a controversial 3–1 defeat at the hands of eventual winners Sheffield Wednesday.

It was not until the 1925–26 season that Arsenal made any further significant progress in Cup competition – though that season was, of course, Herbert Chapman's first in charge. A 2–1 defeat at Swansea City ended that campaign, but the following season the club reached the final for the first time in their history, and though Chapman's first League title at Highbury did not arrive until the 1930–31 season,

Saved... Arsenal goalkeeper Preedy defies Huddersfield in the 1930 FA Cup

interim consolation came with steadily impressive Cup performances.

Wembley winners

The 1927 final, the first to feature radio commentary, saw Arsenal attempting to become the first London club actually to win the Cup at Wembley (Spurs, the only capital side to lift the trophy, had done so at Crystal Palace in 1901 and at Stamford Bridge in 1922). Instead, however, Cardiff triumphed, becoming the only side ever to take the trophy out of England, thanks to a disastrous error by hapless Arsenal goalkeeper Dan Lewis.

On 26 April 1930, the Gunners finally fulfilled their promise, although in that year's semi-final it had looked very unlikely that Arsenal would contest the Wembley showpiece. Hull City were leading 2–0 at Elland Road, and the Gunners were looking alarmingly bereft of imagination.

One quality the side did possess in abundance, however, was determination – the lasting legacy of which can be seen, appropriately enough, in the 1970–71 FA Cup semi-final when Arsenal, trailing 2–0 to Stoke, fought back to level the game on their way to winning the double.

Peter Storey's goalscoring forerunners in 1930 were David Jack and Cliff Bastin, whose heroics earned Arsenal a replay at Villa Park. David Jack's goal was enough to win the game for Arsenal and set up an intriguing final against Huddersfield Town – the dominant English side of the 1920s, and former club of Herbert Chapman.

Arsenal were approaching the end of the season lodged at 12th place in the first division, having taken a very precarious route to the final: Huddersfield looked the more likely to finish in triumph.

Perhaps unsurprisingly, though, it was to be a day of surprises. The first came with the presence of His Majesty King George V at Wembley: the morning newspapers had said he would be too ill to attend, but he upset the odds by making his first outdoor appearance in 18 months. Then it was Arsenal's turn.

The first goal came after a skilfully-worked free kick by Alex James and Cliff Bastin on 17 minutes. James took a quick free kick to release Bastin down the wing, who drew the ball inside for James to lash into the net – a rare goal for the Scotsman, but a strike which fulfilled his pre-match promise to get on the score-sheet.

The remainder of the final saw Arsenal firmly on the defensive, as Huddersfield fought desperately for an equalizer – so desperately, indeed, that when Arsenal managed to clear the ball, with just seven minutes to go, Jack Lambert was virtually on his own in the Huddersfield half, striding on to score the second, clinching goal. The Cup was on its way to Highbury, and Arsenal's – and Chapman's – decade of dominance had just begun.

Disappointment – and disaster

Talk of a possible League and Cup double in the 1931–32 season excited the Highbury faithful – no club had achieved the feat that century – but the two-pronged challenge was to fizzle out in disappointment and controversy.

Everton pipped Arsenal to the League title, while Newcastle inflicted a 2–1 defeat in the FA Cup Final, thanks to a hugely contentious Newcastle goal which levelled the scores after Bob John had put Arsenal a goal ahead.

Newcastle inside-forward Jimmy Richardson was chasing a long clearance deep in the Arsenal half, but as the ball appeared to cross the goal-line, the Gunners defence stopped playing, expecting the goal kick. Instead play continued, with Richardson delivering a cross for Jack Allen to tap into the Arsenal net. Allen later scored another to settle the match.

The 1936 Final gave the club a chance to wipe away the bad memories that remained from their previous visit. More particularly, the players wanted to redeem themselves after the disaster which befell the club on 14 January 1933, another momentous date. That was the day when lowly Walsall pulled off perhaps the greatest giant-killing feat in English footballing history, taking on Herbert Chapman's seemingly-invincible Arsenal side and emerging as comfortable 2–0 winners.

Arsenal entered the game comfortably ensconced at the summit of the League, and having only recently crushed Sheffield United 9–2; Walsall, on the other hand, came into the fixture on the back of three draws and a 5–0 defeat; yet the third-division side overcame the likes of James, Bastin and Jack with revelatory confidence – and, it has to be said, not a little cynical brutality.

The 1936 final thus gave players such as James, Bastin and Hapgood their last tilt at FA Cup glory. A solitary goal from Ted Drake gave Arsenal a victory they perhaps did not really deserve: second-division Sheffield United relentlessly took the game to their more auspicious opponents, and were unlucky to hit the woodwork twice.

Reversal of fortune

For the 1950 final Arsenal were paired with Liverpool, but not before the Gunners had endured an epic semi-final tie with London rivals Chelsea. As had happened in 1930 against Hull, Arsenal conceded two early goals before a slice of extraordinary good luck handed them a ticket back into the match.

Ironically, the goal was scored by outside-right Freddie Cox, who had joined the club from Spurs in September 1949 and thus knew well the White Hart Lane pitch the semi-final was being played on; amazingly, it was scored direct from a corner.

It was a timely strike, coming just before half-time. Arsenal had to wait until 15 minutes from time, however, before Leslie Compton's header from brother Denis's corner finally eased the Gunners' nerves.

The replay was again

Foiled… Ted Drake's challenge on Sheffield United keeper Smith in 1930 is too late

On the way: Arsenal beating Liverpool at Wembley in 1950

staged at White Hart Lane, and again destiny chose Tottenham old-boy Cox to stand centre-stage. Cox's destiny was in fact foreseen by his wife Eileen on the night before the match, when she dreamt her husband would score the winning goal: he duly obliged, although not until the 14th minute of extra time.

In the final, Arsenal's two gambles – to assign Forbes to control Liverpool wing-half Billy Liddell, and to play Reg Lewis up-front – paid off handsomely, with Lewis scoring the two goals which gave Arsenal victory. Joe Mercer finally had his FA Cup medal – although had it not been for the eagle eyes of someone in the Royal Box, Mercer would have taken home a loser's medal instead.

Arsenal returned to Wembley two years later, hoping to regain their hold on the famous silver trophy. Indeed, had it not been for defeats in three crucial matches at the season's climax, Arsenal could have become the first club this century to win the League and Cup double. Instead, as they had done in 1932, they finished as runners-up in both domestic competitions.

To rub salt into the Gunners' wounds, it was again Newcastle who denied them in the Cup Final. This time it took just one goal to settle the scoreline, George Robledo's strike six minutes from the end ensuring Newcastle became the first club to retain the trophy.

The not-so-swinging Sixties

The 1960s saw little to cheer at Highbury, in either the League or the Cup, until the appointment of Bertie Mee in 1966. Within two years, Mee was leading the side out at Wembley, this time in a League Cup final with Leeds United.

Arsenal, like many of the big clubs, had initially viewed the newly-created League Cup with scorn and condescension, only deigning to enter the competition for the first time in the 1966–67 season.

The club's first League Cup adventure was far from auspicious: they lost 3–1 to West Ham after taking three matches to oust Gillingham. The next season saw the Gunners start to rediscover their Cup swagger – though not without some tense moments.

When Arsenal faced Burnley in the 1967–68 League Cup quarter-final tie at Turf Moor the Gunners soon found themselves (not for the first time, nor the last) facing a two-goal deficit. This time, however, the Arsenal response was rapid: two goals from George Graham and one from skipper Frank McLintock gave them a 3–2 half-time lead. McNab ruined the effect in the second half by being sent off, and Willie Irvine plundered a late equalizer for Burnley.

Arsenal scraped through in the Highbury replay, goals from Ronnie Radford and Terry Neill giving them a place in the semi-finals. There they overcame Huddersfield 3–2 in a nail-biting affair – McNab's winning goal eventually proving decisive – to set up a final against Leeds.

The Leeds side, managed by Don Revie, had too often failed to fulfil their potential: they had lost the 1965 FA Cup Final to Liverpool, and twice recently had finished runners-up in the first division.

Against Arsenal, however, their luck finally changed. Arsenal, particularly Mee, were unhappy at the behaviour of Leeds' tallest players, Jack Charlton and Paul Madeley, as a corner swung into the box, but the ball dropped kindly for Terry Cooper to blast into the Arsenal net.

Exactly a year later, Arsenal appeared to have the perfect opportunity to put matters right again. It seemed that all of the hard work had been done after Tottenham had been despatched in the League Cup semi-finals, and third-division Swindon Town awaited in the final.

Double delight... George Graham celebrates Arsenal's opener against Liverpool in 1971

Beware of the underdog

That it was Swindon who nevertheless took the lead on 34 minutes came as a considerable shock – Arsenal had let in only 18 goals in their previous 30 matches, but an uncharacteristic mix-up in defence allowed Smart to tap in for the underdogs. Arsenal were not able to strike an equalizer until Bobby Gould headed past goalkeeper Downsbrough in the 86th minute.

It was Swindon, however, who more readily grasped the nettle in extra time and clinched the glory. After 15 minutes of extra time, and with both sides visibly tiring in the soggy conditions, Don Rogers prodded Swindon back into the lead before scoring again in the second period to put the game firmly beyond Arsenal's reach.

For captain Frank McLintock, this was his fourth trip to a Wembley final, and the fourth time he had been forced to depart a loser. It was fitting, then, that the next time McLintock led his Arsenal team out under the famous Twin Towers of Wembley it would be to the crowning achievement of the club's long history – the FA Cup triumph that clinched the prestigious League and Cup double.

The 1971 FA Cup semi-final against underdogs Stoke, at Hillsborough, again saw Arsenal concede two early goals. As the minutes ticked away in the second half, an improbable reversal of fortunes ebbed ever further into the distance, before Arsenal suddenly broke away after Stoke's Greenhoff had spurned a golden opportunity to score.

George Armstrong fed the ball to Ray Kennedy, who in turn laid the ball on for Peter Storey to strike past Gordon Banks in the Stoke goal. It needed another miss by Greenhoff and two minutes of added time, however, for Arsenal finally to salvage their season. A corner from Armstrong was headed towards goal by McLintock, only for John Mahoney's hands to prevent a certain equalizer. Storey ignored the pressure and the tension to slot home the penalty and guarantee Arsenal a replay, and countless sighs of relief.

Double delight

As had been the case so often in the past, Arsenal wrested the psychological advantage from their hapless opponents. A goal from Graham in the first half, and another from Kennedy in the second, sent Arsenal into the final against Liverpool – their opponents in

Arsenal's last FA Cup victory, 21 years previously.

The final, coming less than a week after Arsenal had been crowned League champions at Tottenham, was bruising and unmemorable – that is, until the inevitable extra-time brought the first goal, when Liverpool's Steve Heighway broke away from the Arsenal defence and squeezed the ball past goalkeeper Bob Wilson. It would need a drastic change of tactics by Arsenal to pull the game back from the brink.

That change came courtesy of coach Don Howe, who ordered George Graham to push up into a more attacking role. Four minutes before half-time of extra time, the additional pressure on the Liverpool defence brought its reward as substitute Eddie Kelly desperately directed the ball towards goal.

With Graham swinging a foot at it, it crept past Liverpool goalkeeper Ray Clemence, and Arsenal were level. Graham raised his arm in celebration, convincing many that the goal was his, although television replays suggest that the future Arsenal boss failed to connect, and the goal should be credited to Kelly.

Not that such details mattered at the time. Once again, the pendulum had shifted, and with just nine minutes on the clock George played a one-two with Armstrong before unleashing a delectable 20-yard shot which flew past Clemence: the 20-year-old forward, who had followed the Gunners as a boy and had come up through the club's youth system, had given Arsenal the Cup, the double and a place in history.

The following May, recent rivals Leeds plundered a single-goal victory to prevent Arsenal from retaining the FA Cup, even though bogey-team Swindon, champions-to-be Derby County, London rivals Chelsea and, once again in the semi-finals, newly-crowned League Cup-winners Stoke City were all knocked out on the way to Wembley.

Had it not been for the Cup competitions, Arsenal's 18-year wait for another League Championship would have seemed even longer. As it was, the record-breaking three successive FA Cup Finals the Gunners reached between 1978 and 1980 were scarcely satisfying, victory only coming in the 1979 fixture.

Tragedy and triumph

1978 saw Arsenal again playing the part of embarrassed fall-guys to less-fancied opposition. Terry Neill led the side out for his first FA Cup Final in charge, but it was Bobby Robson and his Ipswich side who

The winner! Alan Sunderland (left) hails his 1979 strike against Manchester United

emerged hoisting the trophy aloft, thanks to a single goal from Roger Osborne and injuries which rendered Arsenal's Alan Sunderland, Malcolm Macdonald and Liam Brady all less than 100 per cent match-fit.

It was becoming increasingly apparent that the Cup competitions offered Arsenal's most realistic hopes of success: success which finally came the following season, in a final with Manchester United which has gone down as one of the classics.

Not that the first 85 minutes offered much in the way of enthralling entertainment, although Brian Talbot and Frank Stapleton had both scored to give Arsenal what seemed an unassailable lead.

United had other ideas, however, and with time ticking rapidly away first Gordon McQueen and then Sammy McIlroy tucked in scrappy goals which put the game back on level terms. Immediately, the game looked as if it was United's for the taking – a fact Brady seemed to recognize as he carefully controlled the ball in the centre of the pitch, seemingly waiting until extra time.

In an instant, however, Brady had released Graham Rix down the wing and his pinpoint cross was dramatically slid into the net by the onrushing Sunderland. This time there could be no reply from United, and Arsenal were sure of victory – a triumph which made recent signing Brian Talbot only the second player to win consecutive FA Cup-winners' medals with different clubs, having played against Arsenal for Ipswich in 1978.

Here we go... Brian Talbot heads Arsenal ahead against Manchester United

Three in a row

The Gunners' formidable form in the Cup competitions continued in the 1979–80 season, and when Talbot scored the only goal in the third replay of their epic semi-final tie with Liverpool Arsenal had reached a historic third FA Cup Final in succession.

But for the second time in three years they fell prey to the Cup underdogs, this time second-division West Ham, whose solitary goal, headed in by Trevor Brooking, was enough to bring the trophy across London.

Worse was to follow. Only a few years after having been acclaimed as one of the best Cup sides in the country, Arsenal were soon being reduced to a laughing-stock by embarrassing Cup defeats at the hands of smaller clubs.

None more so than Arsenal's League Cup exit at the hands of Walsall on 29 November 1983. What made the second Walsall disaster in the club's history even more distressing was the fact that the Gunners had comfortably beaten Tottenham in the previous round, only to collapse to a lowly third-division side – a club, moreover, who were already an object of loathing in the collective Arsenal memory. Manager Terry Neill lasted barely a fortnight after the 2–1 defeat, but Don Howe's reign failed to bring much improvement.

Indeed, only a couple of months after being appointed, Howe was faced with the wreckage of a 3–2 defeat at second-division Middlesbrough which ended Arsenal's FA Cup hopes at the third-round stage. The following season a 1-0 defeat at fourth-division York City in the fourth round of the FA Cup, followed by a 3-2 Milk Cup reverse at second-division Oxford, continued the alarming trend.

The 1985–86 season saw the Gunners improve slightly, reaching the fifth round in both domestic Cup competitions, but Howe's departure was inevitable, and it was only the arrival of George Graham as his replacement in the summer of 1986 which began to restore the Gunners' winning ways.

In walks Stroller

It was obviously going to take time to create an Arsenal side capable of challenging for the League Championship again. Appropriately, therefore, Graham started steadily but with success. He rounded off a promising first season in charge by inspiring the Gunners to their first silverware in eight years – all the more edifying as the Littlewoods League Cup triumph came against Liverpool, who the previous season had emulated the double-winning exploits of Arsenal and Tottenham.

Unlike their previous League Cup Final appearance back in 1969, Arsenal entered the match as undeniable underdogs, despite pulling off an epic victory in the three-match semi-final tie with Tottenham.

Arsenal were 2–0 down on aggregate at one point before Viv Anderson and Niall Quinn brought them back level at White Hart Lane, forcing a third match. The toss of the coin gave Tottenham home advantage and, with just eight minutes remaining, a goal from Arsenal old-boy Clive Allen, his third of the tie, seemed finally to be sending Arsenal out.

It was then that Ian Allinson, a second-half substitute for Michael Thomas, made his most important contribution in an Arsenal shirt, scoring a precious equalizer: then, in the final minute of the game, David Rocastle scrambled home a winner. Amazingly, Arsenal were in the lead for just one of the 270 minutes the tie had lasted – but unlike their profligate North London neighbours, Arsenal were able to hold on and record a famous win.

At Wembley, however, when Ian Rush put the Merseysiders a goal up on 23 minutes, there was little reason to doubt another piece of silverware was on its way to Anfield – after all, the Reds had never lost a game in which Rush had scored. But then, no one expected Charlie Nicholas suddenly to come up with his most effective intervention for the Gunners.

Champagne Charlie gets the corks popping

Nicholas's days at Highbury were numbered as soon as George Graham arrived as manager the previous summer. Graham the player may have been something of a strutting Jack the Lad – going by the well-known nickname of "Stroller" – but Graham the manager possessed an entirely different attitude, placing key importance on discipline, the work ethic, and, above all, the subordination of individual talent to the collective effort.

Thus the 1987 final was effectively Nicholas's Arsenal swansong: and, ever the mercurial, unpredictable teaser, he finally gave his adoring public something tangible by which to remember him.

Never mind that his first goal, the second-half equalizer, was a scrappy tap-in during a goalmouth scramble, nor that the winner, seven minutes from time, was a mis-hit shot which took a lucky deflection past Grobbelaar: the important fact was that "Champagne Charlie" had finally set the corks popping and brought George Graham a successful finale to his first season in charge.

King Charles: Charlie Nicholas puts Arsenal ahead in the 1987 Littlewoods Cup Final

The Gunners should have been celebrating a repeat performance the following year when they again reached the Littlewoods Cup final, only this time as firm favourites in the clash with Luton Town. Arsenal's progress to the final had seen them score 15 goals and concede just one in seven games, including a 4–1 aggregate win over defending League champions Everton in the semi-finals.

Luton's preparation, on the other hand, had been far from ideal. Their season had threatened to crumble before their eyes, with a 2–1 FA Cup semi-final defeat by Wimbledon closely followed by a 4–1 trouncing at the hands of struggling second-division side Reading in the final of the Simod (lower divisions) Cup.

Luton and pillaging

Nevertheless, it was Luton who took an early lead, Brian Stein hitting the net after only 15 minutes. Even this jolt did little to rouse the Arsenal players into effective action, until Martin Hayes replaced Perry Groves on the hour mark.

Immediately Arsenal began to pose more of a threat down the wings, and with 15 minutes left they seemed finally to have turned the game around: first Hayes prodded home an equalizer, then, five minutes later, Alan Smith steered the ball past Andy Dibble to give Arsenal the lead.

The drama was not over yet, however, and for once Arsenal became the victims, rather than the perpetrators, of an astounding comeback. Indeed, the Gunners should have put the game firmly beyond Luton's reach; Smith headed against the bar and Hayes, a yard from goal, hit the post with the rebound, before Nigel Winterburn was presented with a golden opportunity to seal victory when the Gunners were awarded a generous penalty, for a foul on Rocastle.

In the blink of an eye, however, and to the incredulity of the watching Arsenal multitudes, the penalty rebounded from a post, and was on its way back towards the Arsenal goal. A stumble by rookie defender Gus Caesar compounded the Gunners' confusion, and Danny Wilson struck an equalizer with just five minutes left on the clock.

But still Luton were not satisfied, and with just one minute of normal time remaining, Ashley Grimes managed to break free of the disconsolate Arsenal defenders, who allowed his cross to be flicked home for Stein's second goal of the match.

Graham's work at the club was obviously making great strides, however, as the following year the Gunners snatched their first League title in 18 years. Still, defeat by arch-rivals Tottenham in the 1991 FA Cup semi-final – the first to be held at Wembley – was a more than usually bitter pill to swallow, despite the sweetener of the Championship trophy which was on its way to Highbury within the month.

Wrexham wrecks 'em

If the Tottenham defeat was a particularly unpleasant disappointment, however, the following season's FA Cup campaign was farce and horror-story rolled into one. In the previous season Arsenal had finished top of the League, while Wrexham had finished at the very bottom – but when the champions made their trip to North Wales for the third-round tie, they returned home on the back of one of the biggest Cup upsets of the century.

As in the 1988 Littlewoods Cup final, Arsenal held

Medal Man: Steve Morrow's winner against Sheffield Wednesday in the 1993 Coca-Cola Cup Final

the lead with just eight minutes remaining, thanks to a typical goal from Alan Smith. But the guard suddenly slipped once more, and after Mickey Thomas had lashed a free kick past Seaman for the equalizer, there was still time for Steve Watkins to exploit a chaotic mix-up between the usually-dependable Adams and O'Leary – and the League champions suddenly had to face up to a season in tatters.

It says a great deal for the Highbury spirit, and in particular George Graham's yearning for success, that the Arsenal players roused themselves from the debris of the Wrexham debacle to go on and make Cup history the following season.

It was not a classic Highbury side, and there were incipient murmurings of discontent among Arsenal fans about the failure to relaunch a realistic push for the League championship, but the unprecedented achievement of winning both domestic cups, as the Gunners did in the 1992–93 season, earned Graham's Arsenal another unique place in the history books.

What made the feat all the more unusual was that the unfortunate Sheffield Wednesday provided the opposition in both finals – although the feeling of déja vu may have deterred some supporters, resulting in a disappointing FA Cup Final crowd of 62,267. Nor were those who did make that trip to Wembley blessed with the most inspiring of spectacles.

Indeed, it was the earlier final (now going by the name of the Coca-Cola Cup), which offered the most open and attractive entertainment. John Harkes, the first American to play in a Wembley cup final, gave Wednesday an early lead, but a quick riposte from Man of the Match Paul Merson was followed, in the second half, by an opportunistic winner from young Northern Ireland utility man Steve Morrow.

Unfortunately Morrow, and the match, were made more memorable by the chaotic post-match celebrations, when Arsenal captain Tony Adams dropped the goalscoring hero, breaking his arm and denying him the chance to collect his well-earned medal until 27 days later, when the two clubs met again in the FA Cup Final.

A score to settle

Before then, of course, Arsenal had settled an old score at the semi-final stage by once again meeting Spurs in a Wembley semi-final, but on this occasion there was no Gascoigne, no Lineker, and no early goal to open up the game, and Arsenal emerged as victors, thanks to a headed winner from Tony Adams.

This time it was Arsenal who entered the final as favourites, despite doubts over the fitness of Ian Wright, who had recently suffered a broken toe. Wright, in typically irrepressible fashion, still managed to score in both the first game and the replay – this was, after all, the man who had recovered from a broken leg in 1991 to come off the bench and score two match-saving goals for Crystal Palace in their final against Manchester United.

Unlike those days, however, when his goals were not quite enough to take the trophy, Wright's contribution in an Arsenal shirt was the launch-pad the uninspired Gunners needed.

In the first game it was David Hirst who hit a second-half equalizer for Wednesday; in the replay it was newly-crowned Footballer of the Year Chris Waddle; and as the second game sleepwalked through another extra time miasma it seemed the FA Cup Final would be settled for the first time ever by a penalty shoot-out.

Cometh the hour, cometh the man – although any Hollywood scriptwriter would have been derided for proposing Andy Linighan as the last-gasp hero. Since his £1.25 million move from Norwich in July 1990, Linighan's main function had been as a stop-gap replacement for either Tony Adams or Steve Bould.

The reckless bravery with which he flung himself – broken nose and all – at a 119th-minute corner, however, won him an unforgettable instant of glory when his header hit the back of the net and wrapped up Arsenal's double Cup triumph.

It was a last-minute victory ranking alongside the most dramatic in Arsenal's history: a heist of the highest order which condemned the luckless Wednesday to a barren season.

Graham must have known that his Arsenal side were looking a little creaky and needed some major summer surgery, but for the moment glory and a place in history were his: not only was it the first time a club had won both domestic trophies in the same season, but also the first time anyone had won all three domestic honours – the League, the League Cup and the FA Cup – both as a player and as a manager.

That FA Cup success was not Graham's last silverware as Arsenal manager – glory in the European Cup-winners' Cup, arguably his greatest triumph, was still a year away – but it was the club's last domestic trophy to date.

Disappointing Cup exits at the hands of first-division sides Bolton and Millwall in seasons after 1992–93 left unsightly dents in Graham's highly-polished Highbury machine, and his successor, Bruce Rioch, was denied a place in the 1995–96 Coca-Cola Cup final by an away-goals defeat to eventual winners Aston Villa.

Better late than never... Andy Linighan's 1993 FA Cup Final replay winner

The Premiership Stars

The players who won the League Championships in 1989 and 1991 laid the foundation for the team's assault on the remodelled league.

Tony **Adams**

George Graham took a bold move in March 1988 when he made 21-year-old Tony Adams Arsenal captain, but in the years that followed, it proved one of his most inspired decisions.

Adams, the formidable rock on which Arsenal's defence has been founded for the past decade, has gone on to become the most successful captain in the club's history.

After coming to prominence in the 1986–87 season, when he collected a League Cup winner's medal as well as the PFA Young Player of the Year Award, Adams has built up an impressive haul of accolades and honours – and has come to characterize Arsenal Football Club itself.

It was back in November 1983 that Adams, at the age of 17, made his League debut in the Arsenal colours, after emerging as a trainee at the club, and he was soon winning rave reviews for the composure

Tony Adams made his League debut at 17 and rose to become captain of club and country

and reliability he invariably brought to the back-four.

He was just 20 when he made his international debut against Spain in February 1987, but it is only in the last couple of years that he has established himself as an essential fixture in the England line-up. During Euro 96, however, he erased the memory of a disappointing European Championship in Sweden in 1988 by captaining his country with inspirational intensity.

But it is the Gunners who have benefited most from Adams's presence on the pitch. In addition to the League Championship triumphs of 1989 and 1991, Adams held aloft the FA and Coca-Cola Cups in 1993 and the European Cup-Winners' Cup in 1994.

Injury at the end of last season prevented him from leading the side in the Championship run-in, but as a leading figure in Arsène Wenger's Highbury revolution the skipper shows no signs of easing his commitment.

In fact, under Wenger's more adventurous direction, Adams has been rejuvenated, his more attacking role reflected in a spectacular goal against North London rivals Tottenham at Highbury.

A charging, formidable Tony Adams is sure to be the central core of Arsenal's success for a few more years to come.

> **Tony ADAMS**
>
> **Born:**
>   10 October 1966
> **Position:**
>   Defender
> **Height/Weight:**
>   6ft 1in/12st 1lb
> **Club:**
>   Arsenal
> **League appearances:**
>   391(+4)
> **League goals:**
>   27
> **International caps:**
>   45 (England)

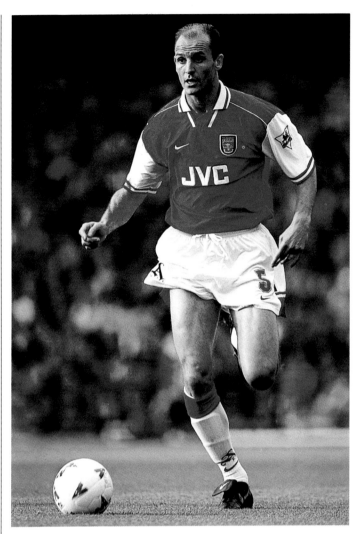

Steve Bould: a bargain buy from Stoke City for £390,000 in 1988

Steve **Bould**

Many people were surprised when Terry Venables gave Steve Bould an England call-up in 1994, at the age of 31.

But the two caps Bould won, against Greece and Norway, were a recognition of the reliable solidity the centre-back had unfailingly provided for Arsenal.

Indeed, Bould partnered Gunners team-mate Tony Adams in central defence, bringing to the England back-four the characteristic Arsenal security.

The England call-up came just a few months after Bould had been a part of Arsenal's Cup-Winners' Cup triumph over Parma. That victory in Copenhagen was particularly sweet for Bould, coming a year after a thigh injury had ruled him out of both the Coca-Cola and FA Cup finals.

Despite the injury problems that have disrupted his partnership with Adams during recent seasons, Bould has been one of the club's stalwart servants since joining from Stoke City for £390,000 in 1988. The 1996-97 season saw him complete his 200th League appearance in the Arsenal colours.

In Bould's first season at Highbury, he picked up a League Championship medal, and when the side again won the title in 1991, Bould added the

> **Steve BOULD**
>
> **Born:**
>   16 November 1962
> **Position:**
>   Defender
> **Height/Weight:**
>   6ft 2in/11st 13lb.
> **Clubs:**
>   Stoke City, Torquay
>   United (loan), Arsenal
> **League appearances:**
>   427 (+8)
> **League goals:**
>   5
> **International caps:**
>   2 (England)

Supporters' Club "Player of the Year" accolade to his collection.

Like Adams, Bould's height and physical power make him a daunting barrier for opposing forwards to overcome. He can also provide an unsettling presence in the opposition penalty area, as the target of the Gunners' set-piece moves.

Kevin **Campbell**

Kevin Campbell enjoyed a remarkable run of success during his time with Arsenal.

He joined as a trainee in 1986, and was the club's youth team top-scorer in both 1987 and 1988.

In 1988 he collected an FA Youth Cup-winner's medal, and was a member of the 1990 Combination-winning reserves side.

It was also in 1990 that Campbell gained promotion to the first team, after brief loan spells at Leyton Orient and Leicester City.

It was not long before he had emerged as a major young talent at Highbury, and he hit nine goals in 22 games on his way to pocketing a League Championship medal. His tireless work connecting the midfield and the attack, and his keen eye for goal, made him an ideal foil for Ian Wright in the Gunners' forward line.

His talismanic taste for success continued with the double-cup triumphs of 1993 and the Cup-Winners' Cup win in 1994. But the intense competition for places at Highbury, particularly after the arrival of Dennis Bergkamp in the summer of 1995, convinced Campbell to look for a new challenge.

Nottingham Forest stepped in with a £2.5 million move, although Campbell's progress has been hindered by an unfortunate run of injuries throughout his two seasons at the City Ground. Certainly, Campbell's lengthy absences throughout the 1996–97 season were a major contribution to Forest's eventual relegation. Campbell will be desperate to spearhead the side's return to the Premiership, a level of competition to which he has become accustomed.

Campbell's explosive breakthrough at Highbury tends to mask the fact that he still has plenty of years left in his career. Whether he can recapture the success he enjoyed at Arsenal, however, when he also received England "B" and Under-21 international call-ups, remains to be seen.

Kevin CAMPBELL	
Born:	4 February 1970
Position:	Forward
Height/Weight:	6ft/13st 1lb
Clubs:	Arsenal, Leyton Orient (loan), Leicester City (loan), Nottingham Forest
League appearances	105 (+38)
League goals:	42

Kevin Campbell: from Youth Cup-winner to Cup-winners' Cup-winner

Paul **Davis**

For so long the model of Arsenal's midfield, Paul Davis never won the England recognition his passing skills deserved, but his time at Highbury brought him a haul of medals few players could match.

Davis joined as a trainee, and made his debut at Easter

Paul Davis (right) brought poise to the midfield

1980, in a North London derby against Tottenham.

His calm poise on the ball and insightful creativity made him a fans' favourite, and his role in the side took on even greater importance when Liam Brady left for Italy.

Although he was called into the England squad on a number of occasions, ill-fortune and injury always prevented him from making an appearance.

Still, he went on enjoying success in the Highbury line-up, winning the Littlewoods Cup in 1987, the League title in 1989 and 1991, the Coca-Cola and FA Cups in 1993 and the Cup-Winners' Cup in 1994.

The curtain came down on a glorious Highbury career in 1995, with Davis recognising that although his control and ball skills remained as impressive as ever, the passage of time was slowing him down.

The emergence of a host of new young midfielders, making an impact in the way Davis himself had done a decade earlier, meant that Davis could leave the club for London neighbours Brentford, his skills and commitment gone but not forgotten.

Paul DAVIS	
Born:	9 December 1961
Position:	Midfielder
Height/Weight:	5ft 10in/10st 13lb
Clubs:	Arsenal, Brentford
League appearances	331 (+20)
League goals:	30

Lee **Dixon**

Lee Dixon has been another of the main beneficiaries of Arsène Wenger's first season in charge at Highbury.

A fixture in the back-four which had been the basis of Arsenal's recent successes, there were suspicions that Dixon might be increasingly limited to a role on the sidelines.

But Wenger's tactical shifts, nurturing a more attacking philosophy throughout the side, have encouraged Dixon to make more adventurous forays down the right wing and into opposition territory.

Lee DIXON	
Born:	17 March 1964
Position:	Defender
Height/Weight:	5ft 9in/10st 12lb
Clubs:	Burnley, Chester City, Bury, Stoke City, Arsenal
League appearances:	320 (+4)
League goals:	20
International caps:	21 (England)

Lee Dixon: settled down at last with Arsenal, his fifth club

Dixon had always impressed as a right-back who enjoyed pushing forward, his ability to cross the ball well with either foot making him a vital part of many Arsenal attacks.

He was well suited, then, to the alterations in attitude and formation that Wenger quickly introduced at the club, managing to combine forward-looking flair with a typical defensive strength.

Dixon joined from Stoke in a £350,000 deal in

January 1988, five months before Steve Bould made the same journey from the Potteries to North London. The transfer generated a useful profit for Stoke, who had paid Bury £40,000 for his services in 1986, after the Manchester-born player had received free transfers from both Burnley and Chester.

The ease with which Dixon settled into to the Arsenal side soon brought him an international call-up, making his debut against Czechoslovakia in April 1990. Although his international career now looks over, after 21 games and one goal in an England shirt, Dixon looks ready to continue his Gunners service in the pursuit of yet more honours.

John **Hartson**

A weight of expectations was placed on the shoulders of John Hartson when he became the country's most expensive teenager in January 1995.

George Graham paid £2.5 million to take the 19-year-old Welshman from Luton Town to Arsenal, placing his faith in the potential the big, red-haired striker had demonstrated in the lower divisions.

It was to be one of Graham's last Arsenal signings, but the seven goals Hartson scored in the 15 games he played that season provided an early glimpse of the talent he possessed.

It was Hartson who scored Arsenal's goal in the 1995 Cup-Winners' Cup Final against Real Zaragoza, a strike which typified Hartson's predatory instincts.

Although Arsenal lost that match, Hartson's involvement rounded off a momentous season for the youngster. Two months after his move to Highbury he won his first full Wales cap, lining up against Bulgaria in a European Championship qualifier.

Unfortunately, the 1995–96 season was not so successful for Hartson, with the presence of Ian Wright and Dennis Bergkamp in the Arsenal front line frustrating his hopes of regular first-team football. He was limited to just 16 starts in the Arsenal line-up, although his power and height made him a useful substitute to have available.

It was the desire for a guaranteed starting-place, however, which convinced him to accept a move across London in February 1997, joining West Ham United in a £5 million move.

His first goal for the Hammers came in a vital win over Tottenham, and his newly formed partnership with Paul Kitson helped Harry Redknapp's side stave off relegation. Hartson's youth means he will have plenty of chances to remind Arsenal of the goalscoring talent they allowed to pass through Highbury.

John HARTSON
Born:
5 April 1975
Position:
Forward
Height/Weight:
6ft 1in/14st 6lb
Clubs:
Luton Town, Arsenal, West Ham United
League appearances:
43 (+10)
League goals:
14
International caps:
5 (Wales)

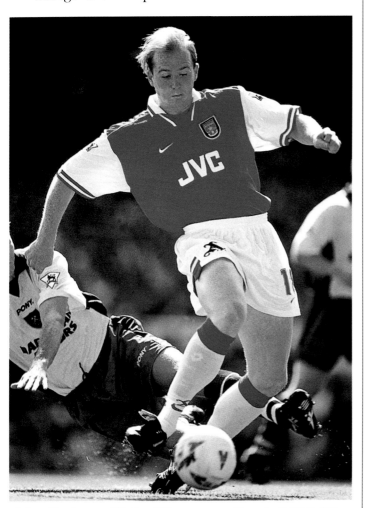

John Hartson: £2.5 million sensation in 1994–95, sold to West Ham in 1997

David **Hillier**

David Hillier's emergence in the 1990–91 season marked him out as a possible future England international. He certainly brought an assurance and maturity to the Arsenal midfield which belied his young age.

Like Kevin Campbell, he was a member of the 1988

Youth Cup-winning team, captaining the side. Also like Campbell, he was to find his progress in the first team frustratingly limited by injuries and competition for places.

His stamina and ability to tackle hard and win the ball in the centre of the pitch made him a useful team player, and he established himself as a regular during the 1991–92 and 1992–93 seasons.

David HILLIER

Born:
18 December 1969
Position:
Midfielder
Height/Weight:
5ft 10in/11st 6lb
Clubs:
Arsenal, Portsmouth
League appearances:
82 (+22)
League goals:
2

A spate of injuries denied him just reward for his talents, however, keeping him out of the two Cup finals in 1993 and the Cup-Winners' Cup final in 1994. The championship medal he won in 1991 was his only major honour at the club.

By the time Hillier had fully recovered from his injuries, the arrival of David Platt and Dennis Bergkamp, and the reinvigorated form of Paul Merson, meant that his first-team appearances were infrequent.

A move to Portsmouth helped him revitalize his career, and Hillier won rave reviews for the displays which took the South Coast club to the FA Cup quarter-finals in 1997, and to the brink of the play-offs. The composure with which Hillier moves with the ball at his feet, from defence to attack, brings to the Portsmouth midfield the unmistakeable legacy of his Highbury upbringing.

Martin **Keown**

Martin Keown's career has seen him go a long way, only to come home at last.

He joined Arsenal as a trainee, making his League debut for the club in November 1985. But after making only 22 first-team appearances, with a loan spell at Brighton, he was transferred to Aston Villa in June 1986 for a fee of £200,000.

Keown's versatility, which enabled him to play at centre-back, right-back, left-back, or even in midfield, soon brought him to the attention of other clubs, and in 1989 he moved to Everton for £750,000. While at Goodison, Keown received his first England cap, in the 2–0 victory over France in February 1992. The

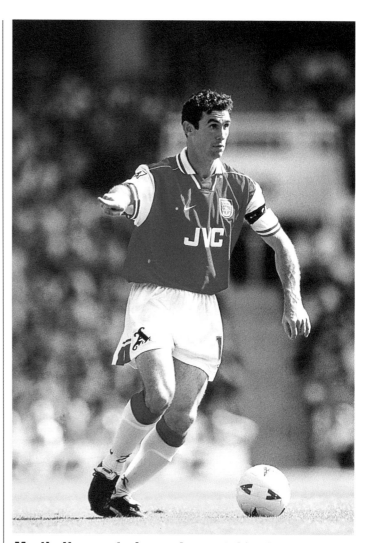

Martin Keown: trainee who cost £2 million to bring home to Highbury

following month he scored a spectacular goal in the 2–2 draw with Czechoslovakia, the first of his three strikes in England colours.

Keown's love for his first club, however, tempted him back to Highbury in February 1993. The £2 million fee Arsenal had to pay out represented a significant increase on the amount for which they had first released him.

At times, Keown has seemed dogged by bad luck in his second spell at

---

Martin KEOWN

Born:
24 July 1966
Position:
Defender
Height/Weight:
6ft 1in/12st 4lb
Clubs:
Arsenal, Brighton and Hove Albion (loan), Aston Villa, Everton, Arsenal
League appearances:
151 (+18)
League goals:
2
International caps:
11 (England)

the club. He was cup-tied for the FA Cup and Coca-Coca Cup finals in 1993, injured for the 1994 Cup-Winners' Cup triumph, and his appearance in the 1995 final against Zaragoza was cut short by another injury, suffered in a clash of heads.

The 1996–97 season, however, saw Keown revitalised, establishing himself as a permanent fixture in the Gunners' new-look defence and reigniting his international career.

When the Arsenal man was called into the squad for the friendly with Mexico, England coach Glenn Hoddle was only the latest person to declare himself an admirer of Keown, after Arsène Wenger had handed him the Arsenal captaincy in Tony Adams's absence and the Gunners' supporters had voted him the club's Player of the Year.

Andy **Linighan**

Andy Linighan cuts an unlikely figure as a goalscoring hero, but he wrote his name into the Arsenal history books with the last-gasp goal which won the 1993 FA Cup.

The Wembley replay against Sheffield Wednesday was heading for a penalty shoot-out. The two sides stood level at 1–1 late in the second half of extra time, when the big centre-back stuck his head out at an Arsenal corner and diverted the ball into the net.

The goal stunned Wednesday, but made it a delirious climax to the season for the Arsenal players, supporters, and, in particular, Linighan himself.

After joining the Gunners from Norwich in 1990 for a fee of £1.2 million, Linighan proved himself a vital member of the Arsenal squad.

During the title-winning 1990–91 season, he played a major role, standing in for Tony Adams at the hub of the defence, continuing the long Arsenal tradition of tall, powerful centre-backs, adept at controlling the ball and stifling opponents.

The oldest of three footballing brothers, Linighan

Andy LINIGHAN

Born:
18 June 1962
Position:
Defender
Height/Weight:
6ft 3in/12st 6lb
Clubs:
Hartlepool United, Leeds United, Oldham Athletic, Norwich City, Arsenal, Crystal Palace
League appearances:
107 (+17)
League goals:
5

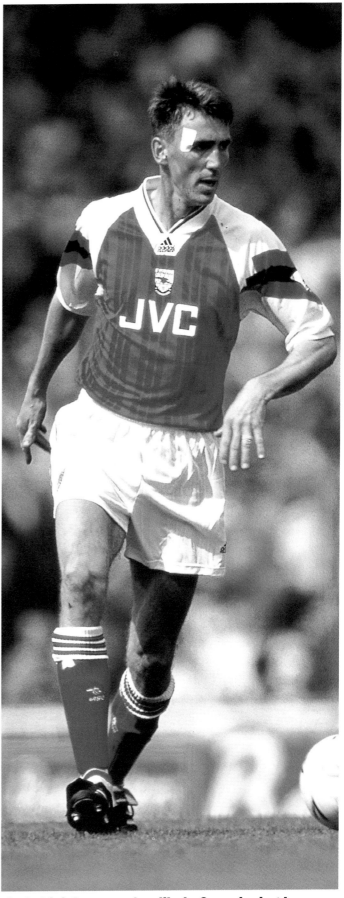

Andy Linighan: most unlikely Cup-winning hero against Sheffield Wednesday

began his career at Hartlepool, his home-town club, before having spells at Leeds United and Oldham Athletic.

Following a £350,000 move to football's top flight with Norwich, Linighan's commanding form thrust him into the limelight. His pivotal role in helping the Canaries achieve their highest-ever League position – third in 1989 – won him the admiration of George Graham, who set up an appetising transfer to Highbury the following season.

After seven years of crucial service to the club, Linighan was released in 1997. Nevertheless, his immortal place in the catalogue of Arsenal magic moments is assured.

Paul Merson

Paul Merson exemplifies the Arsenal reputation for fighting back against the odds and snatching victory from the jaws of defeat.

In November 1994, when Merson made a public confession of his battles against cocaine, alcohol and gambling addictions, the instinctive reaction was to assume that his top-flight career was over.

But the support of the FA, and his club, encouraged Merson to undergo an intensive rehabilitation pro- gramme, and when he made his return to the Arsenal side it seemed that his playmaking talents and incisive

Paul Merson: a delight to watch and an example of how personal problems can be overcome

skills sparkled even brighter than before.

Another of the young prodigies to rise up through the Arsenal ranks, Merson had made many people sit up and take notice after his League debut in the 1986–87 season.

In the years which followed Merson flourished, whether he was playing on the left or right flanks of midfield, or even in a central striking berth.

A Championship winner's medal was won in 1989, followed by another two years later; but it was in the 1993 Coca-Cola Cup final that Merson took a starring role, scoring the stunning first goal in a 2–1 victory on the way to being voted undisputed Man of the Match. Just a few weeks later, he added an FA Cup-winner's medal, and a year later took part in the Cup-Winners' Cup success.

His personal problems, though, threatened to upset the roll of success which had also catapulted him into the England team. But it says a lot for Merson's determination and love for the game that he emerged from this bleak period of his career, not only to win back his place in the Arsenal line-up, but to revel so confidently in his floating role just behind the attack.

His unexpected renaissance was completed when England coach Glenn Hoddle called him back into the national squad during the 1996–97 season. To be pulling on an England shirt, two years after his career had been shrouded in controversy and uncertainty, signified a remarkable turnaround in Merson's fortunes – though his future would have to be away from Highbury following his £5 million move to Bryan Robson's newly relegated Middlesbrough in the summer of 1997.

Paul MERSON
Born:
20 March 1968
Position:
Midfielder/Forward
Height/Weight:
5ft 10in/11st 9in
Clubs:
Arsenal, Brentford (loan), Middlesbrough
League appearances:
289 (+38)
League goals:
78
International caps:
14 (England)

Steve **Morrow**

April 18, 1993 is a date which will be forever etched on the memory of Steve Morrow.

It was Morrow's winning goal which took the Coca-Cola-sponsored League Cup to Highbury, as Sheffield Wednesday fell to a 2–1 defeat. But it was Morrow who bizarrely broke his arm in the after-match jubilation, when unsuccessful attempts by his team-mates to hoist the hero aloft turned the celebrations sour.

Had it not been for Lee Dixon's suspension, after a red card in the recent FA Cup semi-final against Tottenham Hotspur, it is doubtful whether the Belfast-born 22-year-old would even have started in the Wembley final.

But if he thought his Cup-winning goal had impressively staked his claim for a regular first-team spot, then his freak injury quickly punctured these hopes.

Instead of savouring his moment of glory, Morrow was consigned to the sidelines for a lengthy spell, falling back down the Highbury pecking-order.

His versatility, particularly as a midfield marker, meant he was a useful squad-member. His luck returned again when he stepped into the 1994 Cup-Winners' Cup side at the last minute and picked up a winner's medal for his services.

The value of his skills, nurtured since he joined Arsenal as a trainee in 1987, was recognised by Northern Ireland manager Bryan Hamilton, who gave Morrow his first cap in May 1990, later making him captain of his country.

When former Arsenal coach Stewart Houston took over as QPR manager in the 1996–97 season, he remembered Morrow's talents, and made him his first signing. Now fully recovered from injury, no Arsenal fan would begrudge Morrow the chance to taste glory again – this time without the pain.

Steve MORROW
Born:
2 July 1970
Position:
Defender/Midfielder
Height/Weight:
6ft/11st 3lb
Clubs:
Arsenal, Reading (loan), Watford (loan), Barnet (loan), Queens Park Rangers (loan), Queens Park Rangers
League appearances:
39 (+14)
League goals:
1
International caps:
19 (Northern Ireland)

David **O'Leary**

Every side has a player who, through his service and commitment through the years, comes to represent the club and its continuity.

For Arsenal, David O'Leary was that player. In an Arsenal career spanning 18 seasons, from 1975 to 1993, O'Leary made 722 appearances for the Gunners, including 557 League games. Just as it

David O'Leary: pillar in central defence for both Arsenal and the Irish Republic

became hard to imagine an Arsenal side without O'Leary shoring up the defence, it became virtually impossible to imagine the Irishman in any shirt other than the Arsenal red.

If anyone needed further proof of O'Leary's deep-rooted commitment to the club, it came in the tears that flowed from the big centre-back when Arsenal clinched the Championship at Anfield in 1989.

For a man who had made his Gunners debut at the age of 17, in August 1975, it was the ultimate triumph, the only domestic trophy O'Leary had not yet won.

When he emerged in the mid-1970s, it quickly became apparent that the Gunners had an immensely promising defender on their books. At the age of thirteen he had been rejected by Manchester United, but the Gunners were astute enough not to make the same mistake. Together with young fellow-Irishmen Liam Brady and Frank Stapleton, O'Leary provided the backbone for an Arsenal side which reached three consecutive FA Cup finals, winning the 1979 final in an epic encounter with Manchester United.

O'Leary's form dipped in the mid-1980s after the departures of Brady, Stapleton, and Willie Young, his

partner in the centre of defence. But the arrival of George Graham as manager in 1986, and the emergence of the up-and-coming Tony Adams, reinvigorated O'Leary's career.

The signing of Steve Bould in 1988 suggested that O'Leary's Highbury career was drawing to a close, but he fought his way back into the side in time to take a much-deserved role in the club's title-winning success.

Two years later, O'Leary and Arsenal again took the Championship, and O'Leary's respected presence remained at Highbury for a few more seasons, adding FA Cup and Coca-Cola Cup-winners' medals in 1993 to his FA Cup medal from 1979 and his Littlewoods Cup medal from 1987. The highlight of his international career came in the 1990 World Cup in Italy, when he calmly despatched a match-winning penalty in the Republic of Ireland's shoot-out against Romania.

After his retirement, O'Leary predictably found himself much in demand as a coach, but he chose to link up again with former Arsenal boss George Graham at Leeds United. The guiding inspiration he provided for many young Arsenal players during his long spell at Highbury should serve him well in the next stage of his successful career.

David O'LEARY	
Born:	2 May 1958
Position:	Defender
Height/Weight:	6ft 1in/13st 9lb
Clubs:	Arsenal, Leeds United
League appearances:	522 (+35)
League goals:	10
International caps:	67 (Republic of Ireland)

Ray **Parlour**

Ray Parlour has made a rapid impact since emerging in the Arsenal line-up – and not just thanks to his shock of bright red hair.

Even as he was rising through the ranks, Romford-born Parlour seemed to attract success. He won a South-East Counties title medal in 1991, as well as being part of the Gunners' Floodlit Cup-winning side.

He was a mere 18 years of age when he made his League debut against Liverpool in February 1992, and just 20 when he added a Coca-Cola Cup-winner's medal to his collection in 1993. Whether he is played on the right-hand side of midfield or in the centre, the tenacious, ball-winning zeal which he brings to the heart of the Arsenal side have made him a vital figure. The 1994 Cup-Winners' Cup final against Parma saw him on the substitutes' bench, but a year later, in the game with Zaragoza, his place on the pitch was assured.

His progress at Arsenal has been augmented by a series of impressive performances for the England Under-21 side. When the side won the Under-21 Championships in Toulon in 1994, Parlour was voted Man of the Match.

Recent months have seen him struggle to recapture a regular place in the side as he has been held back by injuries, but his prospects remain bright, so long as he continues to ally tireless hard work with his perceptive passing skills.

Ray PARLOUR
Born:
7 March 1973
Position:
Midfielder
Height/Weight:
5ft 10in/11st 12lb
Club:
Arsenal
League appearances:
101 (+35)
League goals:
6

David **Platt**

After spending four successful years in Italy's Serie A, playing for the famous clubs of Bari, Juventus and Sampdoria, it was going to take a big club and an exciting new challenge to lure England captain David Platt back to England. Arsenal fitted the bill perfectly.

With the simultaneous arrival of Dennis Bergkamp, Platt's signing promised great things for the Highbury faithful. Ever since he had scored a spectacular last-minute winner as a substitute in England's World Cup game with Belgium in 1990, Platt's career had been on an upward spiral.

At that time Platt had been Aston Villa captain, impressing many onlookers as a goalscoring midfielder. The decision to release the young Platt on a free transfer in 1985 was surely one of Ron Atkinson's worst decisions as Manchester United manager. After scoring 60 goals in 152 games for Crewe Alexandra, Villa snatched him for £200,000 before selling him on to Bari in 1992 for a record £5.5 million. Although Bari were relegated the following season Platt scored eleven goals, earning himself a transfer to Juventus, followed by two years at Sampdoria. Speculation mounted throughout the summer of 1995 that Platt, who had by then replaced Gary Lineker as England

captain, would be returning to England. It was Arsenal who secured his services, in a £4.7 million deal. Platt had just proved, in the 1995 Umbro Cup tournament, just how important his goalscoring abilities were to the national side.

His surging runs from midfield, his inspirational leadership and considerable footballing intelligence, made him a noteworthy capture for Arsenal boss Bruce Rioch. Unfortunately,

David PLATT
Born:
10 June 1966
Position:
Midfielder
Height/Weight:
5ft 10in/11st 12lb
Clubs:
Manchester United, Crewe Alexandra, Aston Villa, Bari, Juventus, Sampdoria, Arsenal
League appearances:
54 (+3)
League goals:
10
International caps:
62 (England)

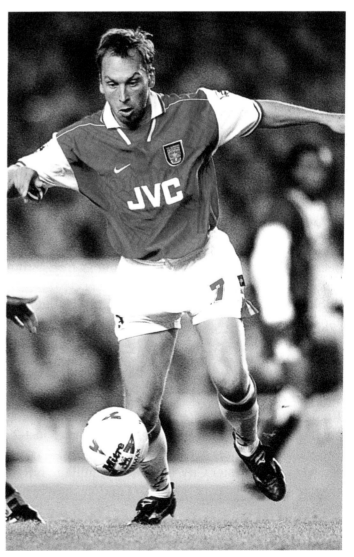

David Platt: returned to England in 1995 with his eyes on the European Championship

Celebration time: Alan Smith is congratulated by Merson and Campbell after his winner against Parma

He is also one of the few strikers to score more than 100 goals in all competitions for the Gunners, a strike-rate which contributed enormously to Arsenal's success during his time at Highbury. Smith retired in 1995, having collected two Championship medals, a Coca-Cola Cup-winner's medal, an FA Cup-winner's medal and a Cup-Winners' Cup medal: a clean sweep of success for the big striker, who also made 13 England appearances in his career, scoring two goals for his country.

The partnership he forged with Ian Wright, after Wright's transfer from Crystal Palace in 1991, gave Smith a new lease of life. From then on Wright would top the goalscoring charts, but Smith continued to weigh in with vital goals, and at vital times. None of them, however, was as vital as his decisive goal on that night of drama in Denmark.

Nigel **Winterburn**

Perhaps George Graham's greatest achievement as manager of Arsenal was not to bring success to the Gunners after so many barren and disappointing years, but to achieve it all without having to splash out ludicrous amounts of money.

Lee Dixon, Steve Bould and Kevin Richardson were all snapped up for bargain-basement fees by George Graham, and Nigel Winterburn, a £350,000 signing from Wimbledon in 1987, was another astute acquisition which has paid off beyond all expectations.

Winterburn was given a free transfer by Birmingham City, his first club, and after a spell at Oxford United established himself at Wimbledon, where he was voted the fans' Player of the Year for four consecutive seasons.

His move to Arsenal brought him to wider attention, as he made the left-back position his own undisputed possession.

His power down the flank meant he became a vital component of attacks, as well as an uncompromising obstacle confronting the opposition's attacks. Winterburn is unlucky to have won only two England caps.

Winterburn also enjoys getting his name on the scoresheet, and provides valuable power at set-pieces – he was, for a while, the club's ever-reliable penalty-taker.

His Arsenal career, has brought him a host of honours, particularly as he has made it his hallmark to miss as few games as possible. Wenger's arrival at the club has allowed Winterburn's attacking instincts full rein, and the sight of the powerful left-back surging down the wing remains one of the crowd's most cherished images.

Nigel WINTERBURN

Born:
11 December 1963
Position:
Defender
Height/Weight:
5ft 10in/10st 7in
Clubs:
Birmingham City,
Wimbledon, Arsenal
League appearances:
345 (+1)
League goals:
7
International caps:
2

Ian **Wright**

Ian Wright's surname makes him a easy subject for newspaper editors keen on clever wordplay – which is convenient, considering Wright is scarcely out of the headlines, for one reason or another.

Happily for Arsenal, Wright is scarcely out of the goalscoring charts either. In each of his five seasons at Highbury, Wright has been Arsenal's top-scorer, and is a perennial contender for the Premiership's Golden Boot award.

Even as time passes and the end of his career is predicted, Wright's boundless enthusiasm for the game, for Arsenal, and for goalscoring effortlessly subdues his critics.

Maybe his desire to keep on going stems from the fact that he entered top-class football at a comparatively late age. His background was in South London local football before he signed for Crystal Palace in 1985 at the age of 21. His attacking partnership with Mark Bright, under the tutelage of manager Steve Coppell, rocketed Palace into the top division, as well as the 1990 FA Cup Final, when a half-fit Wright came off the bench to score two vital goals.

It was in September 1991 that George Graham took out the Arsenal cheque-book, paying £2.5 million to make Wright a Gunner. Wright is not the sort of player who would need time to settle in – in his first season at Highbury he was First Division top-scorer.

Put simply, Wright is a prolific goalscorer. Spectacular or scrappy, on occasions both important and meaningless, Wright's insatiable appetite for glory means he guarantees goals. The FA and Coca-Cola Cup triumphs of 1993 brought him his first major honours, although he missed out on the following year's Cup-Winners' Cup success through suspension. In the 1995 Cup-Winners' Cup campaign, he scored in every round up to the final

Disagreements with Bruce Rioch threatened to bring a premature end to Wright's Arsenal career, but he settled his differences with the club, adjusted seamlessly to the coming of Arsène Wenger, and confounded all those who had predicted his demise by returning to irrepressible form in the 1996–97 season.

Indeed, Wright's goalscoring form was so impressive that he won his way back into the England set-up, at the age of 33. Wright had never previously enjoyed the best of luck in an England shirt, although his appearances were mainly restricted to brief interventions as substitute. But in the summer of 1997 Wright made the most of his return to the England line-up, with goals against South Africa and Italy.

Wright is no stranger to controversy, and his volatile temperament has often threatened to disrupt his career. But the ebullient passions he brings to his game, which make him the target of opposing fans' hate, play a vital role in winning him the devotion of Arsenal fans.

In the 1996–97 season Wright notched up his 100th League goal for Arsenal, and he is fast approaching Cliff Bastin's record of 178 goals in all competitions for the club.

A sign of the respect his talent earned was Wright's "appointment" in the summer of 1997 to head up an FA promotional campaign.

Ian WRIGHT

Born:
Burn: 3 November 1963
Position:
Forward
Height/Weight:
5ft 10in/11st
Clubs:
Crystal Palace, Arsenal
League appearances:
195 (+7)
League goals:
118
International caps:
20 (England)

Ian Wright: late starter who turned into one of the Premiership's sharpest finishers

The Premiership Managers

The post of Arsenal manager is one of the most prestigious in world football. The man in the hot seat benefits from the weight of tradition and respect earned by the legacy of Herbert Chapman. But he also carries the weight of comparative expectation.

Since Chapman and his successor, George Allison, Arsenal has looked for its managers among men steeped not only in football but in respect for the club and its traditions.

Not all have been equally successful. Tom Whittaker, in charge in the early post-war years, had worked his way up at the club under Allison. Later, in the 1950s, Jack Crayston and George Swindin were former players who wanted nothing but the best for the Gunners, but were unable to achieve it.

Neither was Billy Wright – at the time, the most respected of England's just-retired footballers. But it was under Wright that Bertie Mee came up through the ranks of the backroom staff – and it was Mee who revived all Arsenal's dormant pride with the double of 1970–71.

Herbert CHAPMAN

Birth/death:
1873–1934

Career:
Player: Tottenham Hotspur, Northampton Town

Manager: Northampton Town as player manager
Leeds City
Huddersfield Town
Arsenal

Honours:
1924 League championship (Huddersfield)
1925 League championship (Huddersfield)
1927 FA Cup runners-up (Arsenal)
1930 FA Cup winners (Arsenal)
1931 League Championship (Arsenal)
1932 FA Cup runners-up (Arsenal)
1933 League Championship (Arsenal)
1934 League Championship (Arsenal)

Chapman, who had taken his first steps in professional football as an inside forward with Arsenal's historic rivals, was banned from all football activity in October 1919 amid the fallout from the financial scandal which resulted in Leeds City being expelled from the Football League and subsequently disbanded. Chapman worked in a local factory pending his reinstatement by the FA whereupon he took over as manager of Huddersfield Town. He died in March 1934 from pneumonia with Arsenal well on the way to their League titlein four seasons.

Later came Terry Neill, assisted and then succeeded by coaching guru Don Howe. Neill had come from Tottenham Hotspur – and it was to another London club that Arsenal went in 1986, when the time came to rebuild for the era which would see the Premiership explosion. The man for the challenge? George Graham.

George Graham

George Graham achieved more than any other manager in Arsenal's history before his sensational dismissal on 21 February 1995, following an illegal payments scandal.

His roll of honour in his nine years in charge at Highbury included two League Championships, one FA Cup and two League Cups, in addition to the European Cup-winners' Cup. Of course, the likes of Herbert Chapman and George Allison did not have as many titles to aim for – just the championship and the FA Cup in their inter-war day – but Graham's achievements are no less remarkable.

Graham, from Bargeddie in Lanarkshire, was a Scotland schoolboy international. He began his career as a forward with Aston Villa, then moved to Chelsea, with whom he landed a League Cup-winners' medal, before joining Arsenal in 1966. The swap deal sent Tommy Baldwin in the opposite direction.

It was at Highbury that Graham enjoyed the best years of his playing career, first as a striker in the 1968 and 1969 League Cup Final sides and then, thanks to the football intuition of Don Howe, as a midfielder. It was in

League of his own... manager George Graham with the Championship trophy in 1991

George GRAHAM

Born:
  30 November 1944, in Bargeddie
Playing career:
  Aston Villa
  Chelsea
  Arsenal
  Manchester United
  Portsmouth
  Crystal Palace
Honours:
  Scotland (12 caps)
  European Cup-winners' Cup 1994 (manager)
  League championship 1971 (player) 1989, 1991 (manager)
  FA Cup 1971 (player), 1993 (manager)
  League Cup 1987, 1993 (manager)
  Promotion from Division Three 1985 (manager)
Managerial career:
  Crystal Palace (coach)
  Millwall 1984–86
  Arsenal 1986–95
  Leeds United 1996–

---

this role that Graham anchored the 1970 Fairs Cup win and the double the following season.

After another Cup Final appearance, in 1972, Graham moved to Manchester United, and wound down a career which also included 12 Scotland caps with spells at Crystal Palace and Portsmouth.

It was with Palace, at Selhurst Park, that Graham launched his coaching career, and after a stint at Queens Park Rangers he launched out into managership at Millwall. He guided the Lions away from relegation in his first season and then gained them promotion and a secure place in Division Two, before rejoining Arsenal as manager in May 1986.

In his first season, he transformed the club's finances and won the Littlewoods-sponsored League Cup. In 1989, he celebrated a championship as manager to add to the title medal he won as a player in 1971 – then repeated the feat two years later. In 1993 Graham led Arsenal to a historic first – winning the FA Cup and the League (now Coca-Cola) Cup in the same season. One more year and he had conquered Europe, too, as Arsenal beat holders Parma to lift the Cup-winners' Cup in Copenhagen.

But already the tide was beginning to turn. It was also in 1994 that Graham became implicated by the Norwegian agent Rune Hauge in the "bungs" scandal which would eventually bring him down. Hauge gave Graham £400,000 after the transfers to Arsenal of Denmark's John Jensen and Norway's Pal Lydersen.

More than a stroll: Graham outpaces Chelsea's Marvin Hinton in a League match in August 1970

Graham insisted the money had been a mere gift of gratitude. But Arsenal, the media and a Football Association disciplinary commission took a different view and in June 1995 he was banned for a year for misconduct.

Not until September 1996 did Graham return to football – as manager of Leeds United, in succession to Howard Wilkinson.

Stewart Houston

Stewart Houston was the obvious choice to step into the breach after the shock departure of George Graham, having been first-team coach since 1990.

The knowledge he gained on his scouting missions had played an important role in Arsenal's 1995 Cup-winners' Cup triumph, and it was under Houston that the Gunners returned to the final the following season – only to lose amid last-minute drama to Zaragoza in Paris.

As a player, Houston had begun with Chelsea before moving on via Brentford to Manchester United. A steady, dependable full-back, he duly progressed to Scotland international status while building his own reputation.

Houston helped United win the 1975 second-divi-

sion title and collected an FA Cup runners'-up medal the following season. Unluckily he missed out on United's 1977 Cup Final victory because he was injured a fortnight before Wembley.

Stewart HOUSTON

Born:
 28 August, 1949, in Dunoon, Argyll
Playing career:
 Chelsea
 Brentford
 Manchester United
 Sheffield United
 Colchester United
Honours:
 Scotland
 Second Division Championship 1975 (player)
 League championship 1991 (assistant manager)
 FA Cup 1993 (assistant manager)
 League Cup 1993 (assistant manager)
Managerial career:
 Colchester United (player/coach)
 Plymouth Argyle (coach)
 Arsenal (reserve team manager, assistant manager, caretaker manager 1995)
 Queens Park Rangers 1996–97

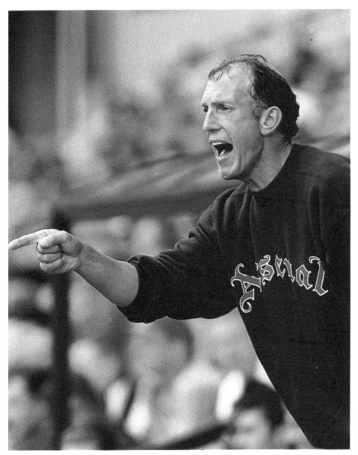

Caretaker supreme: Stewart Houston barks out his orders during a 2–1 win at Leicester

Subsequently he wound down his playing career with Sheffield United and Colchester. Houston's next step on the coaching ladder was at Plymouth, before he joined Arsenal as reserve-team coach in 1987. He became Graham's assistant in 1990.

Houston returned to his assistant's role after the arrival of Bruce Rioch, and then took over as caretaker for a second spell in the autumn of 1996 following Rioch's abrupt departure. When it became clear Houston would never be considered for the top job permanently, he left to launch his own solo career in management, across London at Queens Park Rangers. Pat Rice stepped into the breach pending Wenger's arrival from Japan.

Bruce Rioch

When Bruce Rioch was appointed as the new boss of Arsenal in the summer of 1995, he was hailed as the perfect choice to restore discipline and order to the Gunners' dressing-room. The son of a Scots Guardsman who had been born to the sound of drill-sergeants at Aldershot military barracks, Rioch had the reputation of showing

zero tolerance to players who stepped out of line.

Rioch, a Scotland international midfielder, had started out with Luton Town and hit the heights at club level with Aston Villa and then Derby County before moving on to Everton. He missed out on the 1974 World Cup but captained his country in Argentina in 1978 at the age of 31, finishing his career with 24 caps.

Rioch was not always the most disciplined of players, which taught him a lesson about management. He once said: "Looking back, I know I had a lot of ability and I allowed things to happen which were not necessary. It was part and parcel of the game at that time: over-the-top tackling was commonplace, and if you live by the sword you have to be prepared to die by it. I needed someone to sort me out, to sit me down and tell me it would not be tolerated. As a manager that's what I do." So short hair, uniforms, courtesy, respect and family values became watchwords of the Rioch approach.

Later, in management, Rioch teamed up successfully with his old Derby team-mate Colin Todd. Together, they took Middlesbrough from the the brink of bankruptcy and the third division into the old first division in two years. But then Rioch – alone – left for Millwall, before being reunited in management with Todd at Bolton in May, 1992. The magic was still there; and in their first season, they lifted Wanderers from the old

Ideal choice… or so Bruce Rioch appeared at the time of his appointment

I'm in charge. Bruch Rioch at Highbury on the day he arrived to take over the reins at Arsenal

third division to the Premiership and a Coca-Cola Cup Final appearance.

Liverpool, Wolves, Everton, Aston Villa and Arsenal themselves all fell to Rioch's Bolton in cup competitions, and the Highbury hierarchy were impressed – impressed enough to lure Rioch away as successor to the interim regime of Stewart Houston.

In fact, he was not first choice at the time. Arsenal had originally wanted former England manager Bobby Robson, but that bid hit the rocks when Robson's title-winning Portuguese club FC Porto held him firmly to his contract. Thus Arsenal turned to Rioch.

But somehow, the partnership did not work quite as either side had hoped or intended. Rioch's Arsenal finished fifth in the League, but fell to struggling Sheffield United in the first round of the FA Cup.

Speculation had grown throughout the spring of 1996 that Rioch and the board did not see eye-to-eye over the handling of transfer activities. Rioch and the club had always denied this; but confirmation of irreconcilable differences exploded on the Highbury scene when Arsenal and Rioch parted company at the very start of the 1996–97 season.

Bruce RIOCH
Born:
6 September 1947, Aldershot
Playing career:
Luton Town
Aston Villa
Derby County
Everton
Honours:
Scotland (24 caps)
Managerial career:
Middlesbrough (joint manager)
Millwall (1989–92)
Bolton (joint manager, manager 1994–95)
Arsenal 1995–96
Queens Park Rangers (assistant manager)

Arsène Wenger

Arsenal sprang a major surprise when they appointed Arsène Wenger as team manager in the autumn of 1996. The mutual admiration between club and coach was no secret. But it was still a major step for one of England's major clubs to entrust its fortunes to a foreigner.

Yet Wenger already knew an enormous amount about English football and loves the English game.

That's why he has made no secret of his support for England's bid to host the 2006 World Cup.

As boss of Monaco's French league championship-winning side in 1988, Wenger was considered very much a true son of Alsace – the French region which borders Germany. He was perpetually serious, focused on his football and cautious in his dealings with the media. Like many other French coaches of the era he was also restricted by the intimidating domination of Marseille – by the suspicion that, whatever he taught his players, even he could not keep the occasional corrupting influence at bay.

He once told the London magazine World Soccer: "One of the wonderful things about English football is this passion which people have for their club. That's why every boy has a club loyalty, which is very important as he grows up in the game. It's not the same in France. It's a quality the French game misses."

Wenger has travelled the world following his passion for football, and has long topped the wanted lists of a string of clubs. Only two weeks after he flew to Japan, to take up his appointment as coach of Grampus 8 in Nagoya, he was pursued by Fritz Bohme, president of Werder Bremen, who considered Wenger a potentially ideal replacement for Bayern Munich-bound Otto Rehhagel.

Wenger recalls: "I had to tell them I was sorry, but how could I leave Grampus 8 when I had only just arrived?"

Bremen were too quick, perhaps. By the time Arsenal came along – and Wenger had long been friends with vice-chairman David Dein – he had been in Japan for a year and steered Grampus 8 to the top of the J League. He could move on, confident in the knowledge that he had succeeded in his objective.

The Japanese experience was crucial to the new, relaxed Wenger. He says: "In Japan I learned a lot about myself and how I could be. I was very fortunate to have an experience whereby I was still working in football but outside the European mainstream. All I had to do was train the team. And I found that was what I enjoyed the most – because I did not need to worry about anything else.

"I had a lot of letters, but I could hand them over for some one else to deal with. I could not understand what people were saying or what they were writing in the newspapers, so I did not have that to worry me. I realized that the football was what I enjoyed and the rest was just people's opinions.

"So, since I have come back to European football with Arsenal I take the same approach. I concentrate on the football, on training the team. I can be happy doing that. The rest is not important so I don't let it affect me."

Not that it has been easy for Wenger. In some ways, working in English football – with more experienced, more conservative players – has been harder than it was starting out in Japan.

Wenger says: "In Japan it was much easier to bring something in because professionalism is young, only four years' old. Everything is new – they accept that – and it's more easy to change things. Here, you have 100 years of history. Any time you want to change something, you must convince everybody because of the history.

"Of course, in the tactical knowledge of the players, it's a big advantage, because, tactically, they understand everything. But sometimes to change the habits – and not only at Arsenal, in France it's just the same – it's much more difficult. They say: 'We always did it like this.' What they mean is they don't want to change because they know how difficult that will be."

Diet is one example. Wenger soon altered the players' diets at Highbury. Out went foods such as sugar, red meat and chips, while dairy products were restricted. Definitely in are vegetables, fish, chicken and drinking plenty of water. Players are expected to take part in a spe-

> ### Arsène WENGER
>
> **Born:**
> 22 October 1949, Alsace, France
>
> **Honours:**
> French championship 1988 (manager)
> Japanese championship 1996 (manager)
>
> **Managerial career:**
> Monaco (France) 1986–95
> Nagoya Grampus 8 (Japan) 1995–96
> Arsenal 1996–

cial warm-down after matches, and Wenger brought in a masseur, Mark James. Wenger explains: "I like players to relax with massages and hot baths. I believe they are helpful, physically and psychologically."

In short, sharp training sessions, Wenger introduced a technique called plyometrics which involves much springing, jumping and leaping – designed to enhance players' muscle-power and agility.

The players are happy. They went top of the table under Wenger, and it was not until almost two months after his arrival that they suffered their first domestic defeat, at the hands of champions Manchester United in mid-November.

British players are notoriously superstitious. And

Home from home... Arsène Wenger directs operations on the training ground at London Colney

that's another area Wenger aimed to tackle. He says: "It's not only changing the players. Because, for example, if you go in every day first and take off your left shoe before the right one, and you win, players think you have to go on like that.

"But I'm not really superstitious. I don't have a lucky coat or tie. I fight against that. I think when you really want something a lot, you become superstitious. It's a way to reassure yourself and give yourself some security. But it's a trap, because afterwards you never change your habits."

The former Arsenal striker Alan Smith, now a journalist, summed up Wenger's training changes thus: "I can remember spending two-and-a-half hours on the training field, and 45 minutes would be listening to the manager or the coach talking tactics. With Wenger, I feel he wants to do one exercise after the other. That may leave the players feeling tired, but equally feeling that they have gained something from the work."

Pat Rice, Wenger's assistant, was equally positive, saying: "Arsène has emphasised rest, diet and stretching. The training probably hasn't lasted as long as previously, but it's been very intense. The feedback I get is that our new sessions are demanding, but enjoyable and beneficial too." Top scorer Ian Wright agreed: "Training is a lot more relaxed now. Sometimes, before, it was too regimented. Mr Wenger has completely changed things around, and I am very happy again."

Wenger was equally strong – but flexible – about the way he wants Arsenal to play. His teams usually favour 4–4–2. At Highbury, he has stuck with three at the back, the for-

First impressions: Wenger studying his new team during his first match in charge – a 2–0 victory

mation introduced by Bruce Rioch.

"It's well-known that I like 4–4–2," says Wenger, "but the system must be suited to the players. They look comfortable with the formation we use now."

Under Wenger, fans have learned once again to enjoy watching Arsenal play. Much of this is to do with Wenger's insistence on every player thinking creatively. So Arsenal play through midfield, instead of hitting the ball long to the strikers and using midfielders as mere support players. Patrick Vieira, the young French midfielder Wenger rescued from the reserves' bench at Milan, was one of the outstanding personalities of the 1996–97 season.

Now that he has seen English football at first hand, Wenger is confident it still possesses enormous potential on the European stage. He says: "In England, you have 10 or 11 clubs who can all be among the biggest in Europe. That's unique: it's more than any other country. France has three or four such clubs, Italy five or six, Spain three or four. But because of the love and passion of the people for the game and for their clubs, you have eight or 10 clubs who can be really great."

Of course, plenty of problems remain to be ironed out. Even though he is a new arrival, Wenger appreciates the difficulty of striking a balance between the encouragement of local talent and the need to import "instant" proven ability from abroad.

"The new post-Bosman situation with foreign players has created some difficulties," says Wenger, with his usual quiet line in understatement. "One problem here is that to buy an average player you have to spend too much money – more than the player should be worth. So, naturally, that means clubs bring in more and more foreign players.

"But it's not just an English dilemma. Look at Real Madrid. How many foreign players do they have now?"

Importing foreign players is no simple option for a manager – as Bryan Robson has discovered at Middlesbrough. Wenger adds: "In my opinion, too many foreign players is a problem. Therefore, to equalize the situation, you need free transfers for everyone, both between countries and within countries.

"In Japan, at Nagoya Grampus 8, we had six foreign players but only three could play at any one time. That's not so bad. Initially at Arsenal I brought in two French players (Vieira and Garde). They were well accepted by the English players. But it is not always easy to integrate foreign players if they talk too much in their own language or want to room together on trips. These are factors all coaches have to be aware of. Whatever the individual qualities new players may bring – whether domestic or imported – what matters most is the team. The individual will win nothing unless the team succeeds."

Chapter 7

The Foreign Players

Arsenal have never shied away from difficult decisions in the transfer market. David Jack and later Mel Charles were both domestic record signings in their day. But now, following the landmark Bosman ruling, the world is the Gunners' transfer oyster and few managers have the in-depth knowledge to exploit that as well as Arsène Wenger.

Not that his predecessors were backward in going forward into Europe when good players were available. As far back as 1930 Herbert Chapman had tried in vain to buy the Austrian international goalkeeper Rudi Hiden. It was not until more than 60 years later, however, that foreign talent began to flood onto the field of play at Highbury

Nordic midfielders John Jensen and Stefan Schwarz helped set the tone while Dutchman Dennis Bergkamp remains the foremost figure of world renown to delight the fans after his sensational capture from Internazionale of Milan.

It did not take the Highbury faithful long before they were making the foreign stars feel as much at home as the home-grown talent.

Nicolas **ANELKA**

French football was rocked to its core when Arsenal lured Nicolas Anelka away from Paris Saint-Germain in the spring of 1997.

Anelka had been hailed as the most outstanding attacking prospect in the French game. Paris Saint-Germain expected him to be one of their key players for years to come. However, Anelka was contracted to PSG only as an apprentice – and the club made no attempt to renegotiate his contract.

They had underestimated both Anelka's own ambi-

Young Gunner: 19-year-old Nicolas Anelka was brought in at a snip from Paris St-Germain

Nicolas ANELKA

Born: 14 March 1979
Birthplace: Versailles
Position: Forward
Height: 6ft
Weight: 12st
Signed for Arsenal:
6 March 1997, for £500,000, from Paris St German
Former clubs:
1995 Paris Saint-Germain (Fr)
1997 Arsenal
Arsenal record:
4 apps, 0 goals

tion and the interest his talents had generated abroad. Atletico Madrid had spied him out – and so had Arsenal, thanks to coach Arsène Wenger.

When Anelka turned down Atletico and signed on the dotted line for Arsenal, PSG threatened to lodge a "poaching" complaint with FIFA, the world governing body. Later they had to admit that, under French law, they had no more rights over their own apprentice than any other club at home or abroad.

Dennis **BERGKAMP**

Bergkamp was named after Manchester United's Denis Law and idolized Glenn Hoddle and Spurs as a youngster. But it was Arsenal who fulfilled Dennis Bergkamp's Premiership ambitions.

It took a club record £7.5 million to prise the Dutch striker away from Internazionale of Milan, but with every deft flick, every incisive through-ball and every crisply-struck goal, Bergkamp demonstrates what a world-class talent Bruce Rioch secured for the club.

Amsterdam-born, Bergkamp was named after 1960s Manchester United and Scotland star Denis Law by his soccer-loving father. His name has two "n"s because the registrar would not accept "Denis", claiming it was too much like the girl's name Denise.

The young Dennis soon found himself on the books of local team Ajax, a club boasting one

Dennis BERGKAMP

Born: 18 May 1969
Birthplace: Amsterdam, Holland
Position: Forward
Height: 6ft
Weight: 12st 5lb
Signed for Arsenal:
1 July 1995, for £7.5 million, from Juventus
Career:
1986 Ajax (Hol)
1993 Internazionale (It)
1995 Arsenal
Arsenal record:
61 apps, 23 goals
Honours:
55 Dutch caps
European Cup-winners' Cup 1987
UEFA Cup 1992 (Ajax), 1994 (Inter)

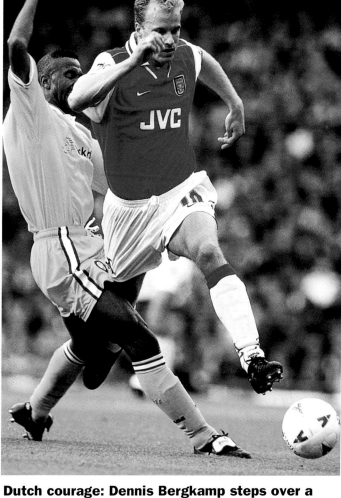

Dutch courage: Dennis Bergkamp steps over a challenge from Leeds' Lucas Radebe

of the most successful youth set-ups in the world. Coach Johan Cruyff gave him his debut at the age of 17 in the 1986–87 campaign in a team featuring his hero Marco Van Basten.

Ajax won the European Cup-winners' Cup that season, Bergkamp making a brief appearance as a substitute in the final against Lokomotive Leipzig.

Initially a winger, Bergkamp was switched into a more central role to great effect. His career really took off from 1990, and he averaged 25 league goals per season in his last three years in the comfortable surroundings of the Dutch league. In 185 games for the Amsterdam club, he hit 103 goals, a phenomenal strike-rate for a player most comfortable playing just behind an out-and-out attacker.

He proved he could perform on a wider stage by helping Ajax defeat Italian clubs Genoa and Torino as they won the UEFA Cup in 1992, and then upstaging

Ruud Gullit and Van Basten when the Dutch reached the European Championship semi-finals that summer. Such displays prompted the inevitable battle for his signature, with Inter snapping up the player for £8 million after he had looked destined either to join Juventus of Turin or to link up with Cruyff again at Barcelona.

Inter won the UEFA Cup in Bergkamp's first season in Italy, but the euphoria which had greeted his arrival quickly turned to disappointment and despondency. Bergkamp found it hard to settle and recapture the form which had won him so much acclaim, and found the net only 11 times in 52 appearances.

His worth as a world-class striker scarcely suffered, however, as long as Bergkamp was still performing outstandingly for the Dutch national side. In particular, goals against England both home and away in 1993 helped ensure Graham Taylor's men failed to reach the 1994 finals.

Any bad feeling David Seaman, David Platt, Tony Adams and Ian Wright harboured towards Bergkamp was forgotten, however, with the Dutchman's move to North London in the summer of 1995.

The grace and fluency with which Bergkamp began to orchestrate Arsenal's attacks bore witness to the presence of a truly great player, and as he and Ian Wright developed a harmonious partnership up-front, Bergkamp started to pay back his fee with interest.

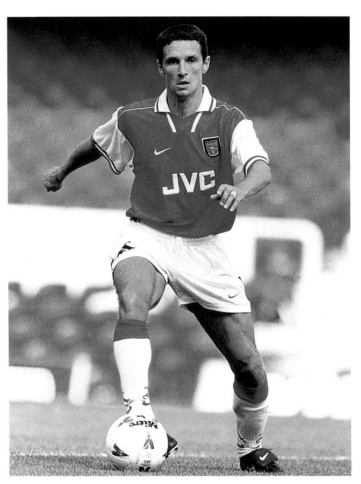

Utility man... Remi Garde can play in defence or in midfield

Remi **GARDE**

Remi GARDE

Born: 3 April 1966
Birthplace: L'Arbresle
Position: Midfielder
Height: 5ft 11in
Weight: 12st 4lb
Signed for Arsenal: 14 August 1996 free transfer from Strasbourg
Career:
1988 Lyon (Fr)
1993 Strasbourg (Fr)
1996 Arsenal
Arsenal record:
11 app, 0 goals
Honours:
6 French caps

Remi Garde was one of Arsène Wenger's first two signings for Arsenal. He had been recommended to the club, along with Patrick Vieira, even before Wenger's official appointment in charge at Highbury. Injury delayed Garde's effective arrival on the Highbury scene but his versatility – his ability to play in the centre of defence or as defensive midfielder – meant he still had plenty to offer.

Glenn **HELDER**

Even before the arrival of Dennis Bergkamp, Arsenal had a Dutch touch in their side after George Graham paid £2.3 million to sign left-winger Glenn Helder from Vitesse Arnhem in February 1995.

Helder's introduction to the Premiership was tentative at first, his involvement largely limited to occasional use as a substitute; but his pace down the flanks, and eagerness to cross the ball quickly, saw him gradually stake a claim for

Glenn HELDER

Born: 28th October 1968
Birthplace: Leiden, Holland
Position: Midfielder/Forward
Height: 5ft 11in
Weight: 11st 7lb
Signed for Arsenal:
14 February 1995, for £2.3 million
Clubs:
1989 Sparta Rotterdam
1993 Vitesse Arnhem (Hol)
1995 Arsenal
1996 Benfica (Por)
Arsenal record
49 apps, 1 goal
Honours:
4 Dutch caps

more frequent appearances.

Helder's ability to adapt to the English game, however, was not helped by his slight build, and his record of only one goal for the club was disappointing for an attacking player.

With the arrival of Bergkamp and Platt, and the conversion of Dixon and Winterburn into more attacking wing-backs, Helder's first-team chances become even more limited, but the enthusiastic flair and exciting style he brought to the side made him a popular figure with the Highbury crowd.

Helder was loaned to top Portuguese club Benfica for the 1996–97 season but was not retained by them.

John JENSEN

It was his goal in the 1992 European Championship Final which brought John Jensen to the attention of many in Europe, but his failure to score was the significant feature of his time at Arsenal.

Jensen eventually broke his duck with a stunning chip against Queens Park Rangers on New Year's Eve 1994, by which time he had become a cult figure to the Arsenal fans.

But his contribution to the side after his £1.1 million transfer from Brondby in 1992 was too easily overlooked by those obsessed with his scoring record. Nestling in the space between defence and midfield Jensen played a crucial anchorman role, picking up an FA Cup-winners' medal in 1993.

He would have added a Cup-winners' Cup medal to his prestigious collection the following year, but an injury suffered while playing for his country ruled him out for the last weeks of the season. This was particularly cruel as Jensen's performances in the European games were among his finest for the club, his brand of commitment and passion ideally suited to

John JENSEN	
Born: 3rd May, 1965	
Position: Midfielder	
Height/weight: 5ft 10in/12st 6lb	
Signed for Arsenal 14 July 1992, for £1.2 million from Brondy	
Career 1983 Brondby (Den) 1988 Hamburg (Ger) 1990 Brondby (Den) 1992 Arsenal 1996 Brondby (Den)	
Arsenal record: 130 apps, 1 goal	
Honours: 69 Danish caps 1988 European Championship 1993 FA Cup 1987 Danish Footballer of the Year	

containing continental opponents.

It was during the 1992 European Championship that Jensen first made his mark on the world stage, as a member of the victorious Danish side which emerged as surprise champions. Jensen's goal in the final against Germany was a particularly memorable strike.

Expectations were high, therefore, when he joined the Gunners; and his lack of goals notwithstanding, Jensen proved himself a capable and admirable team-player. At the end of the 1995–96 season, Jensen returned to Denmark and his former club Brondby.

Anders LIMPAR

Anders Limpar was a frustratingly erratic player, but when he was on form he provided the Arsenal fans with some of the most exciting football witnessed at Highbury.

It was his tendency to drift in and out of matches which eventually persuaded George Graham to let him leave the club, paving the way for a £1.6 million move to Everton in March 1994. But the glimpses Limpar gave of his ingenious ability to bamboozle opposition defenders, deliver crosses of pinpoint accuracy and conjure up goalscoring chances out of thin air thrilled spectators and contributed decisively to Arsenal's Championship triumph in 1991.

It took just £1 million to convince Cremonese to

Super Swede... Anders Limpar sends Crystal Palace's Lee Sinnott the wrong way

Anders LIMPAR

Born: 24 September 1965
Birthplace:
Solna, Sweden
Position: Winger
Height: 5ft 8in
Weight: 11st 5lb
Signed for Arsenal:
6 August 1990, for £1 million, from Cremonese
Career:
1986 Orgryte (Swe)
1988 Young Boys Berne (Swz)
1989 Cremonese (Ita)
1990 Arsenal
1994 Everton
1997 Birmingham City
Arsenal career:
116 apps, 20 goals
Honours:
69 Swedish caps
1991 League Championship
1995 FA Cup

release the Swedish winger in August 1990, after only a year in Italy, but it was a signing which paid off satisfyingly.

Limpar scored 11 goals in his first season at Arsenal, and created numerous others. The arrival the following year of Ian Wright provided Limpar with a more-than-willing target for his creative ingenuity.

Graham, however, felt that Limpar was failing to live up to the brilliance of his early Arsenal displays, and was willing to accept a £600,000 profit on the winger when he sold him to Everton.

Limpar's time at Goodison Park did not bring him the success he had achieved at Arsenal, a spate of injuries leaving his place in the side uncertain, despite his appearance in the 1994 World Cup for Sweden.

For many Arsenal fans, however, the departure of Limpar was a disappointing sight. A player who had sparkled so incandescently on many occasions was lost to the club, and a little bit of magic was gone from the side.

Marc OVERMARS

Marc Overmars is one of the latest big-name signings to grace the marble halls of Highbury – arriving in the summer of 1997 from Ajax Amsterdam with a top-rank pedigree following triumphs in three Dutch championships, the European Champions' Cup and the World Club Cup, plus more than 30 caps for his country.

But Overmars had long since wanted more. His mind was finally made up by events in 1995–96, when knee surgery following a collision in a game against De Graafschap imposed a nine-month lay-off which kept him out of the Champions' Cup Final against Juventus and then the Euro '96 summer showcase in England.

Overmars turned down national coach Guus

New kid on the ball. Arsenal's exciting Dutch winger, Marc Overmars, in pre-season training

Hiddink's invitation to attend the matches – except the 4–1 Wembley defeat by England. Otherwise he preferred to watch the tournament on television while a string of scouts – and reporters – waited for him to prove his fitness.

Overmars told them all: "Of course I'm ambitious. I always wanted to build a career abroad but things were so good at Ajax that I put those plans on hold for a while. Ajax always knew that, at some point, I would want to be let off the leash."

He had joined the Amsterdam club in the summer of 1992 after a season apiece at Go Ahead Eagles and

Marc OVERMARS

Born: 29 March 1973
Birthplace:
Position:
Midfielder/Forward
Height/weight:
5ft 7in/11st
Signed for Arsenal:
Summer 1997, from Ajax
Career:
1990 Go-Ahead Eagles (Hol)
1991 Willem II (Hol)
1992 Ajax (Hol)
1997 Arsenal
Arsenal record:
0 apps, 0 goals
Honours:
34 Dutch caps
1995 European Champions Cup
1995 World Club Champions

Emmanuel **PETIT**

Strongman... ex-Monaco defender Petit

Emmanuel Petit was a target for North London rivals Tottenham Hotspur before Arsenal moved on to the transfer attack in the summer of 1997.

Petit, born in Dieppe but discovered as a teenager by Monaco and brought up through that club's youth system, starred in their league championship-winning success.

He can play in the centre of defence, at full-back or in a midfield holding role. Over the past two years he has successfully turned over a new leaf after a number of brushes with the disciplinary system during his younger days.

Emmanuel PETIT
Born: 22nd September, 1970
Birthplace: Dieppe
Position: Defender/Midfielder
Height: 6ft 2in
Weight: 12st 6lb
Signed for Arsenal: 4 June 1997, for £3 million, from Monaco
Career: Monaco (Fr) Arsenal
Arsenal record: 0 apps, 0 goals
Honours: 15 French caps

Stefan **SCHWARZ**

The interest for Arsenal fans in the Swedish side which finished third in the 1994 World Cup was not reserved for Highbury old boy Anders Limpar.

Just before the tournament began, the Gunners had announced the signing of Benfica's Stefan Schwarz, a regular in the Swedish midfield.

Schwarz had been a member of the Benfica side which triumphed over Arsenal in the 1991–92 Champions' Cup, and fans were excited by the prospect of his ball-winning skills gracing the Gunners' midfield.

Stefan SCHWARZ
Born: 18 April 1969
Birthplace: Kulldall
Position: Midfielder
Height: 5ft 10in
Weight: 12st 6lb
Joined Arsenal: June 1994, for £1.8 million, from Benfica
Career: 1987 Malmo (Swe), 1989 Bayer Leverkusen (Ger) 1990 Benfica (Por) 1994 Arsenal 1995 Fiorentina (Ita)
Arsenal record: 49 apps, 4 goals
Honours 51 Swedish caps

Willem II, and his electric pace and excellent close control created a hatful of goals for team-mates, both with Ajax and Holland – including the crucial 2–2 draw with England at Wembley in the 1994 World Cup qualifying competition.

Travelling man... Sweden's Stefan Schwarz joined Arsenal after spells in Germany and Portugal

His career had begun with his local club Kulldal, before current Blackburn boss Roy Hodgson took him to Malmö. A spell in Germany's Bundesliga playing for Bayer Leverkusen followed, before he moved on to Portugal and Benfica.

Schwarz, however, spent only a year in the Premiership. He adapted well to the rigours of the English League: not only could he win the ball well, but he possessed the vision to distribute it effectively. However, he failed to adapt quite as well to the lifestyle of the English footballer, and moved on to Italy with Fiorentina.

Patrick **VIEIRA**

Injuries are usually bad news for a player and a club – but not when knee ligament damage kept Patrick Vieira out of the French squad attending the 1996 Olympic Games finals in the United States.

The Senegal-born midfielder had to stay at home and was thus missed by all the scouts who flocked to what was, effectively, the world Under-23 championship. Thus Arsène Wenger, not even officially installed as new Arsenal boss, wasted no time in recommending Vieira to his prospective new employers.

Wenger was first impressed by Vieira when the youngster played for Cannes against Wenger's Monaco in the late spring of 1994. Other clubs were also impressed – among them Milan, who amazed their fans by signing this unknown midfielder a year later.

Vieira was hailed by Milan as possibly another Marcel Desailly, but he was kept mainly on the sidelines by coach Fabio Capello, while he learned both Italian and Italian football. Ultimately, he had played only four times for the first team

---

Patrick VIEIRA

Born: 23 June 1976
Birthplace: Angola
Position: Midfielder
Height: 6ft 2in
Weight: 12st 7lb
Signed for Arsenal:
14 August 1996, for £3.5 million, from Milan
Career:
1994 Cannes (Fr)
1995 Milan (It)
1996 Arsenal
Arsenal record:
38 apps, 2 goals
Honours:
5 French caps

Star turn: Patrick Vieira proved an overnight Premiership sensation, with his impressive array of skills

when he suffered his knee injury.

Later Wenger said: "French people feared that, because he missed the Olympics through injury, something must be wrong with him. But I knew he could not be finished at 20. You have to be strong to play in Italy and a young player is not ready.

"In January 1996 I went to Milan to see George Weah collect his World Player of the Year award from FIFA at a big television gala. It was really an accident – George had invited me to go as his guest and said some very kind things about the way I had helped

him. But, as a coincidence, while I was there I happened to meed Patrick. It didn't take me long to realise that he was not happy with his situation there; he had had this injury problem and there were other problems within the club. Anyway, I remembered our conversation later and maybe its Milan now who are not so happy with the way things worked out."

Vieira cost Arsenal £3.5 million but has already proved cheap at the price. As Ian Wright was quick to note: "Vieira makes dream passes for a forward."

And for the fans, as well.

Chapter 8
The Stars of the Future

The Bosman ruling changed clubs' appreciation of transfer values. But the most cost-effective way of developing loyal talent remains the youth development system – as Arsenal have proved many times down the years.

Arsène Wenger's arrival at Arsenal has brought plenty of innovations in the club's behind-the-scenes preparation – new training methods, alternative dietary recommendations – but one thing he has not had to restructure is Arsenal's enviable youth policy.

Arsenal have been perhaps the most consistently successful English club in bringing young players through to first-team action. George Graham's time in charge was an obvious example: he opted to build his success not on expensive signings but on the raw talent already offered by the Highbury playing staff.

Tony Adams, Paul Merson and David Rocastle are just a few of the prodigious talents who flourished when introduced early on to first-team action, all three quickly going on to win international recognition. The side which won the European Cup-winners' Cup in Copenhagen in 1991 boasted six players who had served in the club's youth ranks: Adams, Selley, Morrow, Davis, Campbell and Merson.

Origins of the youth policy

Not surprisingly, the seeds of this approach were planted in the 1930s when Herbert Chapman attempted to take over Clapham Orient, of the third division South, to operate as a nursery club. That ambition was thwarted by the Football League; but in 1934 Arsenal set up Margate, of the Kent League, as an ideal vehicle for testing promising young players in competitive action, under the guidance of former player Jack Lambert. The 17-year-old Highbury hopefuls would be sent down to the coast for five years, 20 at a time, each year costing the club about £6,000 to support. One of the most notable successes was the discovery of Eddie Carr, who scored seven goals in his 11 first-team games in the Championship-winning season of 1937–38.

With the onset of the Second World War, however, the club found itself having to cut back on expenses and the scheme was shelved; and although one of the Margate graduates, Alf Fields, took over in charge of the young squad members in 1951 it was not until the 1960s that the club really began to nurture players effectively again.

Even then, there were considerable drawbacks which only the most enthusiastic coach would attempt to overcome. After the abolition of the maximum wage in 1961 clubs slashed the sizes of their playing staffs. This meant that whereas in the 1950s the teams which Arsenal put out in the Metropolitan and

Striking talent: youth product Stephen Hughes takes on the Everton defence in a 3–1 victory

Combination leagues featured a healthy mixture of young and old, promising and experienced, by the 1970s reserve-team football no longer possessed the same competitive edge and attractiveness. It was then that talented young players began to be loaned out to lower-division sides, rather than have their progress overseen by the club themselves.

Billy Wright's main managerial legacy was to reignite the interest of the Highbury coaching staff in young players' potential, and Arsenal established a reputation as a club passionately interested in the young player as an individual.

Bertie Mee benefited from this more proactive response to up-and-coming apprentices, and the Youth Cup success of 1966, featuring players like Pat Rice and Sammy Nelson, was the launch-pad for the first-team successes of the coming years.

Along with Rice and Nelson, the famous names to emerge from Highbury's homegrown conveyor-belt also include such Arsenal legends as David O'Leary, Frank Stapleton and Liam Brady, the three Irishmen who emerged in the second half of the 1970s, as well as Charlie George, Graham Rix and Paul Davis.

Since Graham took over in 1986, the value of invest-ing in young players has continued to grow. Pat Rice returned to the club as youth team manager and, along with George Armstrong and Youth Development Officer Terry Murphy, has overseen an amazingly pro-lific production-line of Highbury starlets – not only those who, like Adams, Merson and Campbell, have gone on to succeed in Arsenal shirts, but plenty of play-ers who have been sold on to other clubs, netting gener-ous transfer fees.

The decision to let Andy Cole go after just one game may have been a major error of judgement, but the prof-its made from the sales of players such as Neil Heaney, Niall Quinn and Paul Dickov bear witness to the astute preparation and management of young players as part of the Highbury upbringing.

Even with the expensive foreign imports Wenger has brought into the club, it is obvious the manager is not about to disregard the important of the club's local talents.

Wenger's extensive scouting networks are commit-ted to snapping up Europe's most promising youngsters – Nicolas Anelka and Alex Manninger are just two of the exciting prospects for the future brought in from abroad – but his first season in charge also saw the encouraging emergence to first-team action of players who had con-sistently impressed in the youth and reserve teams: Paul Shaw and Stephen Hughes deputised for international stars such as Ian Wright, Dennis Bergkamp and David Platt without showing any signs of being out of place, both players quickly snapping up their first goals in an Arsenal shirt.

Similarly, the future of the Arsenal defence looks secure, with Scott Marshall and Gavin McGowan all looking ready to step into the boots of Tony Adams and Steve Bould whenever needed.

In 1994 Arsenal emulated their predecessors of 1966, 1971 and 1988 by winning the Youth Cup for the fourth time in the club's history, defeating Millwall 5–3 on aggregate – in the first leg, McGowan and Matthew Rawlins scored for Arsenal in a 3–2 defeat, while in the second game, at Highbury, Tony Clarke, Rawlins and finally Hughes got the goals in a 3–0 triumph. Now those players are looking not only to turn out occasion-ally in the first team but to stake their claims for a reg-ular place: Arsenal youngsters have always been given an early chance to show what they can do.

Part of the reason for the instant success such play-ers earn when called up is the characteristic Arsenal emphasis on team spirit and style: players at all levels are brought up on similar principles, playing tech-niques and training practices, guaranteeing the continuity, determination and solidarity which have been staples of Arsenal's success through the years.

Now Don Howe has been brought back to the club to help with youth development, and with Howard Wilkinson newly installed as the FA's first Technical Director, charged with overseeing the production of future England internationals, Arsenal look ideally placed to remain in the vanguard of youth development – so the stars of today are always kept on their toes by the stars of tomorrow.

Arsenal's promising stars of the future to look out for:

Adrian **Clarke**

Adrian Clarke broke into the first team in December 1996, impressing with his ability to play down either flank, providing both pace and accuracy and making him the kind of player who strikers like Ian Wright and Dennis Bergkamp will thrive on. He also

Adrian CLARKE
Born: 28 September 1974
Ht: 5ft 10in
Wt: 11st
Position: Forward
Clubs: Arsenal
League appearances: 4 (+3)
League goals: 0

enjoys scoring himself: Clarke hit the first goal in the second leg of the 1994 Youth Cup Final against Millwall, setting the Gunners on the road to success.

Stephen **Hughes**

The emergence of Stephen Hughes in the 1996–97 season was one of the brightest, if not the most head-line-grabbing, developments during Arsène Wenger's first season in charge. Hughes had already won great acclaim for his performances in the youth team: he played a vital part in the FA Youth Cup success of 1994, scoring four goals in the competition, including one in the second leg of the final. Before the 1996–97 season Hughes had made only one start in the Arsenal first team, but under Wenger he was given the chance to make more of an impact. His useful versatility was

Stephen HUGHES
Born: 18 September 1976
Ht: 6ft
Wt: 12st 12lb
Position: Midfielder/Forward
Clubs: Arsenal
League appearances: 10 (+6)
League goals: 1

demonstrated as he alternately deputised for Dennis Bergkamp, and then Paul Merson, earning himself an extended run in the first team. His first goal for the senior side came in the 2–0 win at Southampton, and the coming years should see him playing an increasingly prominent part in the Arsenal side, following Brady, Davis and Rocastle in the Highbury tradition of homegrown, talented young midfielders.

Scott **Marshall**

Scott Marshall is the most experienced of Highbury's new breed of promising youngsters – his first-team debut came back in the 1992–93 season, and he has

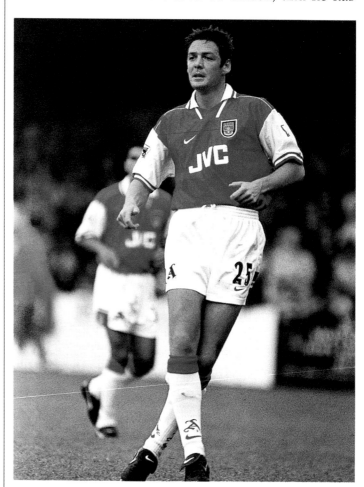

International talent... defender Scott Marshall has represented Scotland at under-21 level

Scott MARSHALL

Born: 1 May 1973
Ht: 6ft 1in
Wt: 12st 5lb
Position: Defender
Clubs: Arsenal, Rotherham United (loan), Sheffield United (loan)
League appearances: 18 (+3)
League goals: 1

already amassed a considerable collection of Scottish Under-21 caps. An unfortunate string of injuries has restricted his first-team opportunities since then but, like the young Tony Adams 10 years ago, he possesses a mature composure in defence that belies his age and experience. What should stand him in good stead over the coming years is his readiness and ability to play the ball sensibly out of defence, as well as appearing at the other end to pose an attacking threat in the air.

Gavin **McGowan**

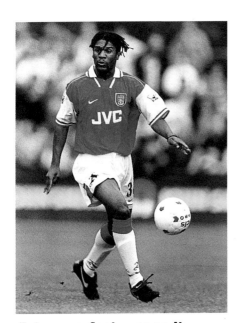

Future perfect... or so it appears for Gavin McGowan

Gavin McGowan's first-team appearances so far have been limited to a few occasions when either Lee Dixon or Nigel Winterburn was missing from one of the full-back berths, but his chance to enjoy a longer run in the side cannot be too far away – particularly as he can play equally well at either right-

Gavin McGOWAN

Born: 16 January 1976
Ht: 5ft 11in
Wt: 12st 3lb
Position: Defence/midfield
Clubs: Arsenal
League appearances: 3
League goals: 0

back or left-back. Another member of the 1994 Youth Cup side, McGowan can also provide vital cover in the both the centre of the defence or in midfield – he scored the second equalizer in the first leg against Milllwall.

Paul **Shaw**

Like Steve Hughes, Paul Shaw marked his arrival in the Arsenal first team by speedily putting his name on the scoresheet. Also like Hughes, he scored in the 2–0 win at Southampton, having already hammered home his first goal for the club after coming on as a late substitute, again against

Paul SHAW

Born: 4 September 1973
Ht: 5ft 11in
Wt: 12st 4lb
Position: Forward
Clubs: Arsenal, Burnley (loan), Cardiff City (loan), Peterborough United (loan)
League appearances: 1 (+11)
League goals: 2

Southampton, in December 1997. After scoring five goals in 14 games while on loan to Peterborough, the chance of a permanent transfer fell through and he returned to Highbury – since when his exciting form has shown Arsenal were lucky to hold on to him. As well as contributing a prolific strike-rate he also offers considerable skill and hard work linking the midfield with the attack, even if so far he has only been able to start one game in the first-team line-up. The 1997–98 season should see him given more of an opportunity to shine than occasional late appearances.

Getting shirty: Paul Shaw holds off a challenge from Southampton's Neil Maddison

Chapter 9

The Great Matches

Arsenal's seasons are never short of drama, whether on or off the pitch, in the League or in Cup competitions.

THE MOST OBVIOUS memories for Gunners fans are the matches which clinched major triumphs: the derby match at White Hart Lane which secured Arsenal the 1970–71 Championship; the 1979 FA Cup Final victory over Manchester United; and, above all, the night of glory at Anfield in 1989, when Michael Thomas's last-gasp winner snatched Arsenal's first League title in 18 years – in the most amazing circumstances imaginable.

The seasons since the beginning of the Premiership have also provided a host of matches which stand out particularly clearly; and although the Gunners may not have recaptured the League Championship they last won in 1991, their efforts against clubs both big and small provided plenty of incident. Whether the man in charge has been George Graham, Stewart Houston, Bruce Rioch or Arsène Wenger, the capacity of the players on the pitch to swing the emotions and excite the nerves has remained an Arsenal trademark.

1992–93

Arsenal fans expecting the side to make a strong start to the new season and reassert their Championship

On the ball: the Arsenal attack during their 2–0 defeat of Liverpool in August 1992

credentials were in for a shock when the Gunners first of all contrived to waste a 2–0 half-time lead on opening day, going down 4–2 at home to Norwich, and then slipped to a disappointing 1–0 defeat at newly-promoted Blackburn. The players needed to rediscover their form in the crunch trip to Liverpool, who had picked up one defeat and one victory from their first two games of the new campaign.

While this 2–0 win could not compare in impor-

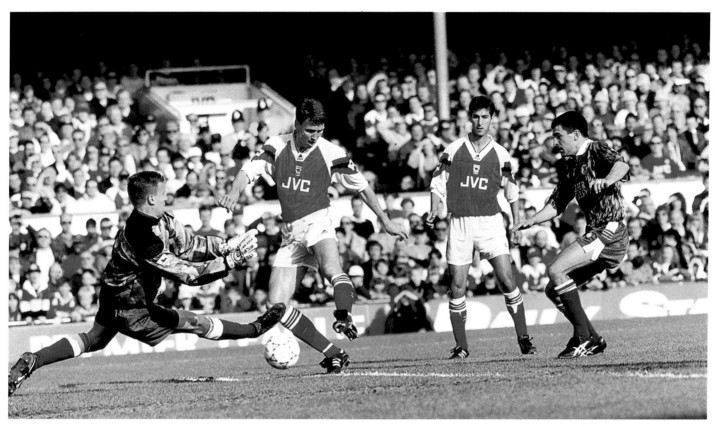

Linighan launches: Andy snatches a rare goal for Arsenal vs Southampton at Highbury in March 1993

---

23 AUGUST 1992

Liverpool (0) 0

Arsenal (0) 2
(Limpar, Wright) *(Anfield)*

Liverpool:
James: Jones (Rosenthal), Burrows, Molby, Whelan, Wright, Saunders, Tanner, McManaman, Walters, Thomas (Marsh).

Arsenal:
Seaman - Dixon, Winterburn, Hillier, Bould, Adams, Jensen, Wright, Campbell, Parlour, Limpar (Merson).

---

tance with the famous Anfield triumph of 1989, it was at least a welcome sign that the Gunners could take on their main rivals and emerge impressively triumphant. Even more encouragingly, young midfielder Ray Parlour, making his first appearance of the season, was at the centre of both goals.

After eight minutes of the second half had been played, Parlour refused to give up when his first attempt at a shot rebounded back off Mark Wright, preventing the ball from going out of play by sending in another cross which goalkeeper David James mistimed, allowing the oncoming Anders Limpar to control the ball and drive it into the net.

The clincher began on the edge of Arsenal's own penalty area, with Paul Merson releasing the ball to Parlour, who in turn fed it through to Ian Wright.

Wright outfoxed Liverpool's attempts to play him off-side and though his shot hit James, it possessed enough power to roll into the net – and Arsenal were back on track for the season.

The Arsenal side which took the field for this fixture had an unfamiliar look to it – there was no Dixon, no Bould, no Jensen, no Smith, and most importantly, no Wright – but those players getting a rare taste of first-team action took part in one of the most memorable games of the League season.

It was Southampton's Ian Dowie who scored the first goal, though, capitalising on early nerves among the makeshift Arsenal defence, before Andy Linighan pacified Highbury by netting a quick equalizer.

Then it was the turn of

---

20 MARCH 1993

Arsenal (3) 4
(Linighan, Merson, Carter 2)

Southampton (2) 3
(Dowie, M Adams, Le Tissier) *(Highbury)*

Arsenal:
Seaman: Keown, Dixon, Davis (Hillier), Linighan, Adams T, Carter, Morrow, Campbell, Merson, Limpar (Dickov).

Southampton:
Flowers: Kenna, Adams M, Hurlock (Dodd), Hall, Monkou, Le Tissier, Cockerill, Dowie, Maddison, Benali (Banger).

one of the familiar faces on display, Paul Merson, to give Arsenal the lead they had expected to enjoy, before the much-maligned Jimmy Carter, making only his fourth start of the season, extended Arsenal's lead.

There was still time before the interval for Southampton to pull a goal back, and show signs that they were prepared to battle for at least a share of the points. Arsenal fans who feared their side would squander their two-goal lead had their anxieties confirmed minutes into the second half, when the Saints' inspirational playmaker Matthew Le Tissier conjured up an equalizer which left David Seaman helpless and the Arsenal defence regretting an afternoon of uncharacteristic laxity.

Salvation was to come, however, in the unlikely form of Carter, whose signing was one of the least successful aspects of George Graham's time in charge.

If conceding three goals was a rarity at Highbury, then at least there was something reassuring in the fact that the winner came from a set-piece: Carter executed the free kick with the confidence of an Arsenal favourite, and a nail-biting afternoon finally came to a satisfying conclusion for the home side, as the final whistle blew on a match which Carter, for one, will not forget.

1993-94

27 NOVEMBER 1993

Arsenal (1) 2
(Wright, Smith)

Newcastle United (0) 1
(Beardsley) (Highbury)

Arsenal:
Seaman: Dixon, Winterburn, Morrow, Bould, Keown, Jensen, Wright, Smith, Merson, McGoldrick.

Newcastle United:
Hooper - Venison, Elliot (Mathie), Bracewell, Scott, Watson, Lee, Beardsley, Cole, Clark (Howey), Sellars.

In the days leading up to this game, the fixture had been transformed from "Arsenal vs. Newcastle United" to "Ian Wright vs. Andy Cole" – an encounter lent extra piquancy by the fact that Cole was returning to the club who had famously released him after just one appearance in an Arsenal shirt.

After having been sold to Bristol City in 1992 for £500,000, Cole had swiftly gone on to confound the Arsenal coaches who deemed him not quite good enough, breaking goalscoring records first for Bristol City and then, after a £1.75 million transfer, for Kevin Keegan's Newcastle United.

Cole's return to Highbury gave him the opportunity to prove emphatically just how wrong George Graham had been to release him. But the other, crucial, part of the equation was the inimitable Ian Wright, seen by many as the "Old Master" to Cole's "Young Pretender".

There was no doubting who would emerge as victor on this occasion, once Wright had applied the vital touch after Steve Bould had nodded on an Arsenal corner. 1–0 to Arsenal, after just 15 minutes, and already a point had been proved to those too quick to proclaim Cole, and too eager to write off Wright.

Cole was kept in check throughout the game by Arsenal's seasoned defence – after all, this was the kind of task Tony Adams and Steve Bould relished. But more of a surprise was the important contribution Bould made at the other end of the pitch.

After having set up Wright's opening goal, Bould performed a similar trick on the hour mark, again nodding on a corner, this time for Alan Smith to convert. Peter Beardsley's goal barely a minute later failed to turn the tide back in Newcastle's favour, and Keegan himself later admitted that Cole "hadn't had his fairy-tale after all".

For Wright, however, as his jubilant celebrations always make plain, every goal in an Arsenal shirt is his own personal fairy-tale – and, as Cole had found out, a Highbury happy ending for one person means disappointment for another.

March was a revelatory month for Arsenal players and fans alike. Perhaps the Gunners had

5 MARCH 1994

Arsenal (3) 5
(Wright 3 (1pen), Youds og, Parlour)

Ipswich Town (0) 1
(Dixon og) (Highbury)

Arsenal:
Seaman: Dixon, Winterburn, Hillier (Keown), Bould, Adams, Selley, Wright, Smith, Parlour, Limpar (Merson).

Ipswich Town:
Baker: Youds, Thompson, Stockwell, Wark, D Linighan (Mason), Williams, Slater, Palmer, Marshall, Kiwomya.

26 MARCH 1994

Arsenal (0) 1
(Merson)

Liverpool (0) 0
(Highbury)

Arsenal:
Seaman: Dixon, Keown, Davis, Bould, Linighan, Jensen (Morrow), Wright (Smith), Campbell, Merson, Selley.

Liverpool:
James: Jones, Dicks, Redknapp, Wright (Nicol), Ruddock, McManaman, Whelan, Rush, Barnes, Fowler (Thomas).

been saving up their goal quotient from October – when they neither scored nor conceded a single goal in all four League games – but in March the goals came pouring out, starting with an emphatic 5–1 victory at struggling Ipswich Town.

Not surprisingly, if goals were on the menu, then Ian Wright would be first in the queue to bag his share, and anyone else's that was on offer too. Ipswich's lacklustre defence was simply overrun by Highbury's "goal-machine", who was obviously straining at the leash after being rested for the previous Wednesday's Cup-winners' Cup quarter-final match in Torino.

After Wright had netted the first after just 18 minutes, the Gunners were always threatening an avalanche. Ipswich's Eddie Youds inadvertantly helped the

Laid back... Ian Wright after scoring for Arsenal vs Newcastle Utd in 1993

Gunners by turning an Anders Limpar cross into his own net six minutes later, and the home defence again contributed to their own downfall five minutes before half-time, when Limpar was fouled in the penalty area. Ian Wright – who else? – inevitably sent the spot-kick ripping into the net, and the Gunners no doubt entered the half-time break speculating on how many more goals they could rack up.

The second half saw two more from Arsenal, with Ray Parlour heading the fourth and Ian Wright completing his hat-trick with four minutes left, outfoxing Ipswich's attempts to play the offside-trap before firing home. In the context of such a decisive victory, Lee Dixon's own goal mattered as little more than

comic relief in the midst of the unrelenting target-practice at the other end of the pitch.

Arsenal were well and truly on the march in the weeks leading up to the Liverpool game. Torino had been beaten in the quarter-finals of the Cup-winners' Cup, and a respectable 2–2 draw with Manchester United had followed spectacular away successes, 5–1 at Ipswich and 4–0 at Southampton.

The form which had taken the Gunners to the semi-finals in Europe, and to fourth place in the Premiership table, had convinced Graham that he could finally get rid of the unsettled Anders Limpar, who was sold on the Thursday before Liverpool's visit, after Everton had agreed to pay £1.6 million for

Heading in... Ray Parlour for Arsenal and Liverpool's Neil Ruddock in action in March 1994

the Swedish winger.

Graham perhaps felt that he could not afford to accommodate two similar players like Limpar and Merson in the same line-up – so while Limpar was settling in at Goodison Park, Merson was scoring the only goal against a Liverpool side sixth in the table.

The Gunners defence was without Tony Adams, but the reshuffled back-four, with Andy Linighan slotted in alongside Steve Bould, coped impeccably with the dangerous strikeforce of Ian Rush and Robbie Fowler, who had provided 32 goals between them already that season. The 19-year-old Fowler was kept so quiet that he was eventually substituted, bringing a

return to Highbury action for Michael Thomas, who had left Arsenal for Anfield in 1991.

After Merson had struck the winning goal in the 47th minute Arsenal were content to ease off and soak up the Liverpool pressure, saving themselves for the following Tuesday's Cup-winners' Cup semi-final with Paris St-Germain – yet another adeptly-managed calculation which was to pay off successfully.

1994–95

February had not yet finished, and already Arsenal's domestic season was virtually over: out of both the FA and the Coca-Cola Cups, and floundering at 12th in the Premiership table.

But what made this midweek, otherwise-unexciting scrap so highly-charged were the amazing events earlier that day at Highbury: George Graham, manager since 1986 and the most successful boss in the history of the Gunners, had been sacked for "failing to act in the best interests of the club" – Arsenal, restored by Graham to successful stability, had once again been cast adrift on a wave of uncertainty.

In the immediate aftermath of Graham's departure, it was his assistant, Stewart Houston, who was entrusted with the manager's job, albeit on a temporary basis. But for fans turning up at Highbury for the game with high-flying Nottingham Forest, the news that Graham was no longer part of the club was dispersed and greeted with stunned incredulity – especially as Graham himself still beamed from the pages of the match programme.

The Highbury crowd chanted Graham's name during the match, and these were still his players on the pitch – the midfield line-up of Jensen, McGoldrick and Schwarz exemplified the hardworking, gritty style of play Graham had instilled in his Arsenal.

Ironically, the match was won by two of the players brought in by Graham as his Highbury

---

21 FEBRUARY 1995

Arsenal (0) 1
(Kiwomya)

Nottingham Forest (0) 0
(Highbury)

Arsenal:
Seaman: Dixon, Winterburn, Jensen, Bould, Linighan, McGoldrick, Merson, Kiwomya, Schwarz, Helder.

Nottingham Forest:
Crossley: Lyttle, Pearce, Cooper, Chettle, Stone, Phillips, Gemmill, Bohinen, Lee, Woan (McGregor).

reign drew to its messy finale – Chris Kiwomya, who scored the only goal, and Dutch winger Glenn Helder, making a sparkling debut after signing for Graham just a week earlier

Kiwomya left it late to put a smile on the fans' faces, however, with the clinching goal coming just four minutes from time. The three points allowed the Gunners some relief after a season of poor performances which had even started to provoke whispers of possible relegation – and to grind out a victory in such circumstances, against a Forest side on the rise, sent out the typical Arsenal message that the individual may have gone, but the collective lived on to prosper: an attitude Graham himself would have appreciated, having done so much to implant it at the club himself.

1995–96

When a club pays £7.5 million for a player – particularly a player renowned as one of the best strikers in Europe – expectations will inevitably be high. Which is why, when Dennis Bergkamp completed his eighth game for Arsenal without scoring, and against lowly Hartlepool United in the Coca-Cola Cup, the media were quick to assault him with such phrases as "expensive flop" and "waste of money".

Bergkamp provided the perfect response in the fix-

Screamer! Bergkamp scores against Southampton in splendid style for his first Gunners goal

---

23 SEPTEMBER 1995

Arsenal (2) 4
(Bergkamp 2, Adams, Wright)

Southampton (2) 2
(Watson, Monkou)
(Highbury)

Arsenal:
Seaman: Dixon, Winterburn, Keown, Bould, Adams, Parlour, Wright, Merson, Bergkamp, Helder.

Southampton:
Beasant: Dodd, Benali (Heaney), Magilton, Hall, Monkou, Le Tissier, Watson, Shipperley (Warren), Maddison, Widdrington.

---

ture with Southampton: not only did he score, but he scored twice, and not only did he score twice, but he scored two stunningly-executed goals, which immediately set Highbury, and his own Arsenal career, sparkling with incandescence.

The first came after just 17 minutes, Bergkamp volleying past Dave Beasant with clinical precision after Glenn Helder had provided a perfectly-placed cross. The jubilation which greeted that strike inspired Arsenal to pursue a more attacking policy than the Highbury fans had been used to.

Tony Adams was the next player on the scoresheet, just six minutes later, heading home after Steve Bould had flicked the ball on. Adams clearly enjoyed taking it upon himself to join in the side's attacks more frequently, having scored twice in the game with Hartlepool – the Arsenal skipper later admitted he was thrilled to hear the fans chanting "Tony Adams on the wing"!

And although Gordon Watson pulled a goal back just a minute later, and Ken Monkou snatched an equalizer on the stroke of half-time, this was destined to be Bergkamp's occasion. Just over 20 minutes later Bergkamp unleashed another shot which crackled through the hapless Southampton defence, past Beasant, and splashed into the net.

Then it was the turn of his new striking partner, Ian Wright, to remind the crowd that he was still there to score goals, too. If Bergkamp's strikes were characteristically stylish

---

21 OCTOBER 1995

Arsenal (0) 2
(Merson, Wright)

Aston Villa (0) 0
(Highbury)

Arsenal:
Seaman: Dixon, Winterburn, Keown, Bould, Adams, Parlour, Wright, Merson, Bergkamp, Helder.

Aston Villa:
Bosnich: Charles, Wright, Southgate, McGrath (Fenton), Ehiogu, Taylor, Draper (Milosevic), Yorke, Townsend, Staunton (Johnson).

strikes, Wright's goal exemplified the persistence and enthusiasm which mark him out as one of the game's top goal-poachers. Wright's attempts to shoot were consistently blocked until, refusing to give up the opportunity of a goal, the single-minded striker found a way through the massed defence to strike Arsenal's fourth of the match, and his seventh of the season.

This time there was no response from Southampton, who had been reduced to the role of passive admirers, as Bergkamp took his bows and left the pitch a new Highbury hero.

Arsenal went into this game on the back of some prolific goalscoring exploits: in their previous match, Leeds had been despatched 3–0 at Elland Road, while the previous week Hartlepool had been trounced 5–0 in the second leg of the second-round Coca-Cola Cup tie.

Even more pleasing for manager Bruce Rioch was the developing partnership between Bergkamp and Wright up-front, with both players starting to contribute goals on a regular basis – as well as being perfect foils for each other. In the last four games, both players had netted five times each.

Aston Villa, however, as Villa old-boy Rioch knew, would be a tougher side to break down – that season, only Leeds had managed to score twice against Brian Little's side. Villa had ended the previous season by only just avoiding relegation, but Little had introduced a new three-man defence, and summer signings Gareth Southgate in defence, Mark Draper in

---

4 NOVEMBER 1995

Arsenal (1) 1
(Bergkamp)

Manchester United (0) 0
(Highbury)

Arsenal:
Seaman: Dixon, Winterburn, Keown, Bould, Adams, Platt, Wright (Hartson), Merson, Bergkamp, Helder.

Manchester United:
Schmeichel: G Neville, Irwin (McClair), Bruce, Keane, Pallister, Cantona, Butt (Sharpe), Cole, Scholes (Beckham), Giggs.

---

midfield and Savo Milosevic up-front were starting to settle in well.

Later in the season, Villa's formidable defence would frustrate Arsenal's attempts to reach the Coca-Cola Cup final, holding out for a 0–0 draw at Villa Park after a 2–2 draw at Highbury – Villa won on away goals, and went on to lift the trophy themselves.

But in the League match at Highbury, it was Arsenal who triumphed, although with the score goalless at half-time, it was becoming increasingly frustrating for the watching Arsenal supporters.

However, they had to endure just two minutes of the second half before Paul Merson, starting to re-establish himself as the central playmaker of the Arsenal midfield after his personal problems, managed to penetrate the Villa ranks and slot the ball past Australian goalkeeper Mark Bosnich.

Villa were unable to produce enough to find an equalizer – the partnership between Milosevic and Dwight Yorke, despite encouraging signs, was still in its formative stages, and the Yugoslav striker's inexperience in the English game was evident as the assured Arsenal defence blocked any attempts on David Seaman's goal.

Inevitably, it was Ian Wright who taught Milosevic how it should be done, clinching the three points with a well-taken goal with just 12 minutes of the match remaining. For Rioch, the match revived old loyalties – to the club he used to play for; to Little, who had been one of his coaches in his time in charge at Middlesbrough – which made the impressive victory all the more satisfying.

Dennis Bergkamp summed it up

That man again: Ian Wright celebrates the second goal as Arsenal go 2 up against Aston Villa in October 1995

On his knees: Peter Schmeichel is soundly beaten by Dennis Bergkamp as Arsenal take the lead

in the match programme, when he said: "The game against Manchester United is the one which will allow us to judge how good we really are."

United undoubtedly were, and are, the major players in the Premiership, and went into the game having clawed their way back to second in the table after a stuttering start to the season. Already Alex Ferguson's side had been knocked out of the UEFA Cup and the Coca-Cola Cup in embarrassing circumstances (to Rotor Volgograd and York City, respectively), but the United line-up were clearly determined to win back the Championship they had ceded to Blackburn Rovers on the last day of the 1994–95 season.

Ferguson's line-up no longer boasted the talents of Mark Hughes, Paul Ince and Andrei Kanchelskis, all of whom had left Old Trafford in the summer: but, ominously for Arsenal and the rest of the Premiership, he could at least pencil in Eric Cantona's name, after the Frenchman had served out his suspension for the infamous Selhurst Park incident.

Cantona had already served notice that he was back, by scoring in his comeback game with Liverpool and by linking up formidably with up-and-coming young talents such as David Beckham, Nicky Butt and

Paul Scholes, who had scored in three of United's previous four games.

Arsenal, however, have never been a side likely to buckle in the face of an opponent's reputation, and if anyone was likely to contain the erratic Frenchman Cantona and his team successfully it would be Rioch's firmly-disciplined, tried and tested, and precise Arsenal back line.

With Adams, Keown and Bould suppressing the menace of the enigmatic French playmaker and Nigel Winterburn and Lee Dixon marshalling the wings with both defensive security and attacking potential, Dennis Bergkamp's 14th-minute goal proved decisive. After kickstarting his Arsenal career with a selection of top-quality strikes, Bergkamp proved he could put away the more mundane chances just as well, nipping into the six-yard box to tuck the ball past Peter Schmeichel.

With David Platt restored to the Arsenal team after a 10-match lay-off through injury, against the side which had released him on a free transfer over a decade ago, the Gunners had made another massive stride in showing, as Bergkamp put it, "just how good we are".

3–1 to the Arsenal... Ian Wright scores his second (Arsenal's third) against Sheffield Wednesday

1996–97

Arsenal, and Ian Wright in particular, celebrated the official announcement of Arsène Wenger's imminent arrival in style – but there was to be plenty of incident, and a selection of surprises, before the Gunners could be sure of victory.

The pattern was set by a power failure in Highbury's East Stand which prevented the turnstiles opening and delayed the kick-off by 27 minutes: when the action did start, the Arsenal players were the ones slow to get into the game and lacking spark.

Wednesday, on the other hand, were obviously keen to return to winning ways after their 100 per cent start to the season had been ended by Chelsea two days earlier.

After 25 minutes 19-year-old striker Ritchie Humphreys continued his prolific start to the new season, latching on

---

16 SEPTEMBER 1996

Arsenal (0) 4
   (Platt, Wright 3 (1pen))

Sheffield Wednesday (1) 1
   (Highbury)

Arsenal:
   Seaman: Dixon, Winterburn, Keown, Bould, Linighan, Platt, Wright, Merson, Parlour (Vieira), Hartson.

Sheffield Wednesday:
   Pressman: Atherton, Nolan, Pembridge, Walker, Whittingham (Trustfull), Hirst, Booth, Blinker (Oakes), Stefanovic (Nicol), Collins.

---

to a through ball from Ian Nolan to slot Wednesday into the lead.

That setback seemingly jolted Pat Rice (still in charge as caretaker-manager until Wenger touched down) to shuffle the line-up, sending on £3.5 million signing Patrick Vieira for his first appearance in an Arsenal shirt.

Almost instantly, the former Milan midfielder made an impression, his poise and passing skills quickly winning him the support of the Highbury crowd, and from then on the Gunners began to claw themselves back into the game. Before Vieira's introduction, Wednesday's David Hirst had seen his volley rebounded off the crossbar. Now it was Arsenal's turn to come close, Wayne Collins clearing off the goal-line from a Martin Keown header, but the visitors went in at half-time still leading.

That lead lasted for 12 minutes of the second half before David Platt crashed home his first goal of the season, after John Hartson had harried Collins off the ball in the Wednesday penalty box.

Arsenal having levelled the scores, the stage was now set for Ian Wright to take his customary starring role. His first goal was a calmly-despatched penalty, after Des Walker had brought down Paul Merson in the area – an offence for which Walker was shown a second yellow card and dismissed.

It looked as though that 2–1 lead would be enough, until the 78th minute when a Lee Dixon cross eluded Merson's lunge only for Wright to arrive in the right

30 NOVEMBER 1996

Newcastle United (1) 1
(Shearer)

Arsenal (1) 2
(Dixon, Wright)
(St. James's Park)

Newcastle United:
Srnicek: Peacock, Albert, Elliott, Gillespie, Batty, Lee (Watson), Beardsley, Ginola, Asprilla (Kitson), Shearer.

Arsenal:
Lukic: Dixon, Winterburn, Keown (Linighan), Bould, Adams, Platt, Wright, Merson (Morrow), Hartson (Parlour), Vieira.

place and slot the ball past the despairing Kevin Pressman.

The whole of Highbury shared with Wright the knowledge that had taken him to 99 League goals for the club – and it was inevitable that Wright would be impatient for the 100th.

When it came, in the very last minute, it was another opportunistic close-range effort, but would have been just as memorable for Wright as the many spectacular goals he has scored in Arsenal colours.

In the immediate aftermath Sheffield Wednesday, still without a League win at Highbury in 34 years, were mere bit-players: no one watching could have doubted that the star of the night was Ian Wright, Wright, Wright.

No doubt Arsène Wenger and his opposite number Kevin Keegan would have asked their players to forget any ill-feeling lingering from the clubs' bad-tempered Coca-Cola Cup tie back in January.

Their requests would have been wasted breath, however, in a match which saw referee Graham Barber book eight players and dismiss Tony Adams.

In the earlier game, United's David Ginola had been sent off after appearing to aim an elbow at Lee Dixon. Adams's dismissal for a professional foul was similarly contentious, with the Arsenal captain protesting that England colleague Alan Shearer made too much of the challenge on him.

Shearer's claim that the foul took place inside the penalty area went unheeded, but there was little mercy for Adams, who made his way to an early bath after just 22 minutes.

Down to 10 men, Arsenal faced an immense task just to try and hold on for a point, with Wenger forced to bring on centre-back Andy Linighan in place of striker John Hartson. Although the Gunners had risen to second in the table Newcastle were top, and enjoyed the passionate support of most of the 36,565 spectators at St. James's Park.

Lee Dixon had opened the scoring on 11 minutes,

converting a Wright cross for his second goal of the season. But two minutes before Adams's dismissal Newcastle had pulled themselves back on to equal terms, courtesy of a Shearer header, and looked the likelier side to emerge victorious.

The pressure on the adjusted Arsenal defence was almost relentless, with Shearer always threatening to put United in front, with support from the obvious attacking skills of Ginola, Peter Beardsley and Faustino Asprilla, although without the injured Les Ferdinand.

But threaten was all that the Newcastle forwards did. For all the attacking strengths of Keegan's line-up there were obvious defensive weaknesses, which were exposed in a classic counter-attacking move which saw Ian Wright race clear to score a 60th-minute winner, his 17th goal of the season.

United looked to Ginola for their inspiration but the French winger's luck was out, with one particularly glorious effort floating just high of Lukic's goal.

The closing stages of the match may not have been pretty – referee Barber flourished the yellow card at Lee, Peacock and Beardsley for Newcastle and Platt, Wright, Dixon, Keown and Merson for Arsenal – but the gritty determination of Wenger's Arsenal ultimately proved more effective than the cavalier flamboyance of Keegan's starry United line-up.

When the final whistle blew to put the Arsenal

5 APRIL 1997

Chelsea (0) 0

Arsenal (1) 3
(Wright, Platt, Bergkamp)
(Stamford Bridge)

Chelsea:
Grodas - Petrescu, Clarke, Burley, Johnsen (Myers), Minto (Nicholls), Parker (Granville), Morris, Zola, Hughes, Vialli.

Arsenal:
Seaman - Dixon, Winterburn, Keown, Bould, Garde, Platt, Wright (Anelka), Hughes (Selley), Bergkamp, Vieira (Parlour).

players and supporters out of their anxious anticipation, Wenger's side had deposed the League leaders – and established themselves at the top of the table instead. It was a position no one could have expected the Gunners to occupy just a couple of months ago – indeed, an hour ago it had seemed extremely unlikely that Newcastle would have been beaten.

But even without Tony Adams, the emblem of Arsenal resolution, the Gunners had shown once again their unfailing capacity for carving out vital victories.

It was an early start for this London derby, the two sides kicking off at 11.15 on a Saturday morning – a novelty not just for Arsène Wenger but also for his Chelsea counterpart, Ruud Gullit.

This clash of London's two Continental managers promised an intriguing array of talents and personalities: Chelsea's line-up, in particular, boasted an assortment of nationalities, and while Roberto di Matteo was unavailable the club's other two Italians, Gianfranco Zola and Gianluca Vialli, were in action.

They must have regretted getting up that early, however, as they endured a disastrous spell in front of goal: Vialli had a particularly miseable morning, completed when his 85th-minute shot hit a post.

By then Arsenal had already coasted to only their second League win at Stamford Bridge in 23 years.

Bergkamp was in no mood to do any favours for Gullit, his former colleague in the Dutch national squad, and set up both Arsenal's first two goals before wrapping up the game himself near the end.

The first goal owed something to luck with a Zola pass taking a ricochet to Bergkamp, who threaded a beautiful pass through the midfield into the path of Ian Wright, who made no mistake in the face-off with Chelsea's Norwegian goalkeeper Frode Grodas.

The start of the second half brought a tactical reshuffle from Gullit, with the Chelsea side reverting to a three-man defence, Andy Myers replacing Erland Johnsen and youngster Danny Granville coming on for Paul Parker, who had been making his first appearance in a Chelsea shirt: ironically, both substitutes were young players Arsenal had allowed to escape from their clutches.

But the effect of the changes was minimal: David Platt waited just eight minutes after the restart to strike only his second League goal of the season, after Bergkamp had provided another inch-perfect pass.

Chelsea had their chances to score, with Vialli and Zola coming closest to beating David Seaman from a 25-yard free-kick; but the most likely player to score was Bergkamp, who got his chance with 10 minutes remaining, when the ball spun into his path after a mix-up between Myers and Craig Burley.

The cool Dutchman rounded Grodas before steering the ball into the empty net with aplomb, taking his season's tally to 13 goals, and five in the last seven games.

The Chelsea players obviously had their minds on the following week's FA Cup semi-final with Wimbledon, and were also missing the suspended di Matteo and Dennis Wise, and the recuperating Frank Leboeuf and Eddie Newton.

But Arsenal had taught their cosmopolitan neighbours a clear lesson about allying deft European intricacy with solid English passion – and earned themselves a satisfying Saturday afternoon off.

Decisive Dixon: Lee heads in the first against Newcastle in an away match that ended 2–1 to the Arsenal

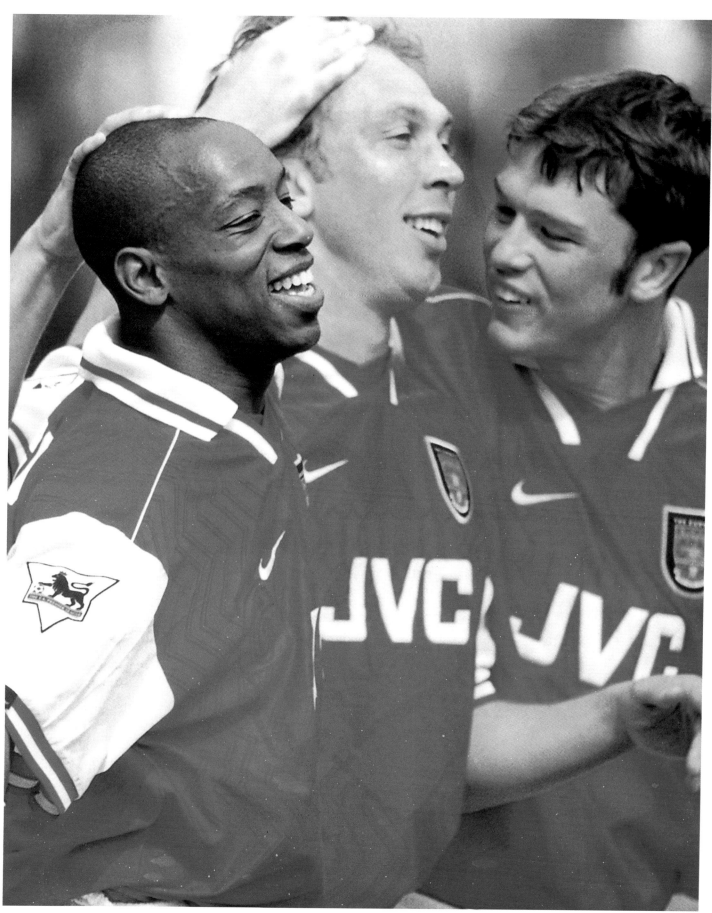

Three for three: Ian Wright, David Platt and Stephen Hughes celebrate as Arsenal win 3–0 against Chelsea

Chapter 10
At Home

The hallowed halls of Highbury are home to one of the world's great clubs – and a worthy stage on which the Gunners have taken on not merely the best of British but the rest of the world.

Stadiums student Simon Inglis once described this corner of North London as "quite simply the most balanced and orderly ground in the country … a symbol of a bygone age, an example of fine architecture, where all lines are in total harmony."

The visitor to Highbury today – if one can get a ticket in these top-capacity, all-seater Premiership days – has no doubt that he or she is sitting in one of the great theatres of soccer. So Highbury does not boast the six-figure capacity of a Bernabeu, a Nou Camp or an Azteca. But it breathes a tradition and a history which go back much further than those great stadia in Madrid, Barcelona and Mexico City.

Not in our back yard

Not that Highbury has always been the most popular site for a football ground. It opened in September 1913, for example, amid a storm of controversy: local residents were hostile to the idea and footballing neighbours Tottenham and Clapham Orient objected vehemently to the invasion by a team from "south of the river".

But Arsenal were here to stay. A string of appeals were fought and lost as the Gunners settled in – later underlining the fact of their arrival, thanks to the shrewd

judgment of Herbert Chapman, by getting the name of the nearby Underground station changed to Arsenal.

Recently Arsenal hit new problems over proposals to expand the stadium. In the summer of 1997 new Sports Minister Tony Banks scuppered ambitious plans to increase seating capacity by 10,000 to nearly 50,000 by having the East Stand declared a Grade II-listed building.

This means that the North Bank Stand, opened in 1993 at a cost of £16.5 million, could be the last major redevelopment at Highbury for a while, particularly since concerns about both circulation of air over the pitch and planning matters means that Arsenal will not be "filling in the corners", as Manchester United have been able to do at Old Trafford.

The original objections to the very presence of a football stadium at Highbury were based on the change of use of the land, which had previously been home to St John's College of Divinity. Apart from opposition from its footballing rivals, Arsenal also fell foul of Islington Borough Council. A petition was compiled against the granting of their lease, claiming that football clubs "exploited footballers for dividend purposes" and that a popular football ground in the area would harm property values.

The grand East Stand

Ironically Islington has, in recent years, metamorphosed into a prestigious area – helped in no small measure by the Tony Blair set. Soaring house prices would have meant the club having to find up to £10 million to buy the 25 houses whose demolition was necessary to the most recent expansion plans.

The East Stand, central to the latest discussions, was designed in 1936 in the Art Deco style by architect William Binnie. It was the finest grandstand of its era and, at £130,000, cost twice as much as the East Stand at White Hart Lane, completed the same year.

Built almost identically to the West Stand – how strange that this has not also been listed! – it was opened in October 1936, and apart from a few alterations has remained the same ever since.

It was during the 1930s that Highbury gained an international reputation to match the team's growing stature as a potent force within the game. This was all a far cry from the playing fields of the divinity college, which needed a mountain of work to make them fit for professional football.

Arsenal had paid £20,000 for a 21-year lease from the Ecclesiastical Commissioners, who insisted that the club should not play home games on Good Friday or Christmas Day. This was revoked in 1925, thanks to the powers of persuasion of chairman Henry Norris.

Kick-off at Highbury

Despite the condition of the fields – the pitch was not even up to standard for the opening match against Leicester Fosse on 6 September 1913 – the new site had two great advantages. Not only was it in a densely-populated urban area: it was also virtually next door to Gillespie Road Underground station – the only ground in London to have been so blessed. It was 20 years later that Chapman persuaded London Transport to rename the station "Arsenal": the company had initially objected, on the grounds that this would have been advertising. The change was ultimately effected on 5 November 1932 – just in time for the opening of the West Stand

The original design for the stadium was provided by Archibald Leitch - one main stand on the East side and three banks of open terracing, his usual format. But the East Stand was vastly different from his previ-

Calm before the storm: Highbury on a match day, full of fans eagerly awaiting kick-off

ous designs in having two tiers, whose extra capacity meant 9,000 seats. The multi-span roof also included the individual letters of the name "Arsenal" painted on each gable front.

Excavation rubble from the underground workings was used to raise the banking by 11 feet at the north end, while it was lowered five feet at the south. On the day of the opening match against Leicester Fosse, the players had to wash in bowls of cold water. One injured player had to be carried away to hospital on a milk float.

Arsenal won that game, and as Christmas approached the seats were completed and conditions were much improved...just in time for the cessation of professional football for the duration of the First World War. Norris, who had invested £125,000 on his own cash in the club – much of it in the stadium – was furious but helpless.

When the war ended in 1918, Arsenal were £60,000 in debt – making it imperative that Norris succeeded in "talking" Arsenal into promotion ahead of Tottenham in 1919. They have never, in nearly 80 years since, been relegated – the longest continuous spell of any club in what is now the Premier League. Whisper it quietly in some corners of North London, but even Tottenham have spent some time out of the top flight in all those years...

Arsenal got in ahead of Tottenham in international terms too. It was on 9 December 1931, that Highbury first hosted a full England international match, ahead of White Hart Lane – thus rubbing more salt into the wounds of Tottenham, who claimed to have more cover and better facilities than Arsenal. The international match in question was a 7–1 thrashing of a Spanish team, complete with legendary goalkeeper Ricardo Zamora. White Hart Lane was not to welcome the senior England side for another two years, when it

Bust of the best: this memorial to Herbert Chapman is in Highbury's marble halls

hosted a game against France which England won 4–1.

Slowly, Arsenal had taken command of their home. Chapman had arrived as manager, the 10-acre ground had been purchased outright for £64,000 and the Ecclesiastical Commissioners had been persuaded to allow the team to play on Good Friday and Christmas Day.

Further redevelopment began in 1931. Local people were asked to bring in their rubbish to build up the banking. One coal merchant backed up too close to a hole dug for the North Bank: both his horse and cart fell in. The horse was so badly injured it had to be destroyed and was thus duly buried under the North Bank.

Money no object

Work began the following summer on the new West Stand which was to become the most advanced and most impressive grandstand in Britain, designed not by Leitch but by Claude Waterlow Ferrier. Completed six weeks ahead of schedule in December 1932 at a cost of £50,000, it was the most expensive stand of its time.

One of its most futuristic features was an electric lift. It also contained seats for 4,000 plus standing room for 17,000 in a simple double-decker arrangement.

Another innovation at Arsenal was the introduction of floodlit football in November 1932 – on the eve of a London conference on the future of floodlit football. Despite the success of the game, the idea was not approved by the FA and Arsenal had to wait another 20 years before using lights "properly".

But Highbury was the focus for another important first – the first televised transmission of an English football game on 16 September 1937 – a practice match, as it happens, specially staged between Arsenal and Arsenal Reserves.

The Second World War saw Highbury adapt to changing circumstances. It served as a first-aid post and an Air-Raid Precautions centre, while the dressing-rooms became clearing-stations for casualties of the bombing. Five incendiary bombs destroyed the North Bank roof and burned up the goalposts. Eventually, wartime football became impossible and Arsenal had to take refuge with their sporting enemies at White Hart Lane.

In due course the Highbury pitch was relaid and the North Bank roof rebuilt with money granted by the War Damages Commission. Always innovative, Arsenal were one of the first clubs to experiment with undersoil heating at an installation cost of £15,000.

Today's visitor to Highbury will see few obvious changes on the outside. The main doors of the stadium are topped off by the AFC motif and the Gunners emblem, while the fabled marble hall – in the main foyer of the East Stand – is dominated by a bust of Herbert Chapman modelled by Jacob Epstein. The bust was commissioned by 12 of Chapman's friends, who would meet each year on 4 January, the anniversary of his death, to talk and lay a wreath on his grave in Hendon churchyard. Elsewhere in the stadium is his carved chapel seat from his church in Yorkshire, presented to him at Easter 1931.

The club even has its own red post-box in the corridor, and upstairs in the boardroom are two small cannon – one of which was said to have been fired before each game in the days of Woolwich Arsenal.

Abundant trophies and memorabilia are exhibited showbiz-style in the guest-rooms and corridors, which are next to – but zealously protected from – the media section, comprising the press room, telephone room, conference room and, of course, the press box itself.

Arsenal's emblem – red on a cream background – features at each side of the stand and the balcony walls are cream with scrolled stonework.

The Gunners: this decoration from the East Stand is part of the whole stadium's classic look

The East Stand has side-towers at each end which house all the touchline facilities. To either side of the tunnel are bench seating for the club reserves and juniors and the managers' shelters. For years, the home team's shelter was always a more homely place since it was fitted with a plug for an electric heater, whereas the away team's had none!

Other features which highlight the Arsenal flair for detail and opulence are the four flagpoles which grace the front of each stand roof and the Gunners' emblem on the side of the stands.

Oddly, the pitch is one of the smallest in London, measuring 110 x 71 yards. This was no problem in the 1930s as far as international matches were concerned, but later developments meant Highbury was ruled out for senior internationals. Thus, during the 1966 World Cup finals, the "other" London region ground – after Wembley – was the now-demolished White City in West London. Size

Man of words: best-selling author Nick Hornby

also counted against Highbury when the Football Association was looking for venues for the 1996 European Championship finals.

Both the north and south ends of the ground have now been completely redeveloped. The North Bank Stand includes a museum, club shop, several restaurants and many fast-food outlets, as well as what Arsenal claim to be the finest toilets in English football grounds. They are certainly some of the cleanest. The money was raised through a controversial bond scheme in the 1980s.

Thus, all in all, Highbury is a home fit for one of football's grandee clubs: a home in which literary lions such as Melvyn Bragg and Nick Hornby can feel quite as much at home as boxer Nigel Benn, actor and TV presenter Tom Watt, presenter and author Clive Anderson, and disc jockey Pete Murray ... and as much as the fan in the street.

Chapter 11

The North London Derby

The Manchester derbies may attract higher attendances, the Merseyside derbies may inspire more entertainment, but there are no more intense clashes in England, or perhaps the world, than when the two North London giants, Tottenham and Arsenal, lock horns.

Title-clincher: Ray Kennedy scores the goal that secures the 1971 League Championship for Arsenal

PERHAPS ONLY THE Celtic-Rangers rivalry boasts a headier brew of bitterness and competition than that of the North London derby – but in the case of Spurs and Arsenal, with none of the sectarian, non-footballing factors coming into play. It is a rivalry born out of football, pure and simple.

And it is a rivalry which goes back a long way: back to 1915, when then-Arsenal chairman Henry Norris artfully manoeuvred a League annual general meeting into accepting Arsenal into the first division – while relegating Tottenham to the second.

The acrimony snowballed as the two clubs both emerged as leading forces in the English game. In 1922 two players were sent off in an ill-tempered North London derby, prompting an FA Commission of Inquiry, while in 1928 Arsenal were accused of throwing games to ensure Tottenham's relegation.

But while the clubs have rarely come face-to-face in battles for major honours – when one is doing well, the other is generally experiencing a spell in the doldrums – some of Arsenal's most memorable successes have involved their old North London rivals playing an important role.

Most famously, the 1970–71 League Championship was actually won at White Hart Lane, a late goal from Ray Kennedy clinching the title on Tottenham's home turf, and prompting wild celebrations from the Arsenal contingent – the Gunners had not only invaded their neighbours' home, but had proceeded to throw their own party there.

The relationship between the two clubs took another interesting twist in the mid-1970s when Terry Neill resigned his job as Tottenham manager to take over on the other side of North London – a move unprecedented in the history of the two clubs. Neill went on to annoy Spurs fans even more by taking with him his assistant, Wilf Dixon, and Tottenham players Pat Jennings and Willie Young, before beating Spurs to the signature of Malcolm McDonald.

Perhaps one of the most spectacular performances of Neill's time in charge at Highbury was the 5-0 defeat the Gunners inflicted on Spurs at White Hart Lane two days before Christmas 1978, with Alan Sunderland smashing a hat-trick.

The most memorable derbies of recent years have been the three epic Cup ties of the past decade. In the 1986–87 season, Arsenal eventually emerged triumphant after a three-match Coca-Cola Cup semi-final tie with their old enemies, only taking the lead for the first time in the last minute of the third match.

Then, in 1991, the two clubs were drawn against each other in an FA Cup semi-final for the first time. The FA broke with tradition by staging the game at Wembley Stadium where, despite Arsenal's pre-match billing as favourites, a stunning Paul Gascoigne free kick from 30 yards after just two minutes, followed by a Gary Lineker goal seven minutes later, swept Spurs to a famous 3–1 victory.

Revenge came two years later when the two sides returned to Wembley, and the Premiership clashes between the old enemies have seen a similar process of counter-balanced fortunes – with both sides, you can only expect the unexpected.

1992–93

The first North London derby of the Premiership could not have come at a worse time for the Gunners. Three consecutive defeats had seen them toppled from the top of the table without scoring a goal, and Paul Allen's first-half goal was enough to compound the

---

**FA PREMIER LEAGUE
12 DECEMBER 1992**

Tottenham Hotspur (1) 1
(Allen)

Arsenal (0) 0
(White Hart Lane)

Tottenham Hotspur:
Thorstvedt; Austin, Edinburgh, Samways, Mabbutt, Ruddock, Howells, Durie (Barmby), Nayim, Sheringham, Allen.

Arsenal:
Seaman; Lydersen, Winterburn, Hillier, Bould, Adams, Jensen (Limpar), Wright, Campbell, Merson, Parlour.

---

misery. Graham's side slipped to eighth as a result, while Tottenham edged up a place to thirteenth.

Scoring goals was obviously a problem for Arsenal: the Tottenham defeat came in the middle of a run which saw the Gunners score just one goal in seven games, inevitably by Ian Wright.

History repeated itself when Arsenal and Tottenham were drawn together to contest an FA Cup semi-final and, as they had done two years earlier, the FA decided to stage it at Wembley.

That is where the similarities with the 1991 game ended, however, with no Gascoigne or Lineker to provide the spark for Spurs, and Arsenal determined to close the game down more than they had done in that 3–1 defeat.

The result was a much tighter, cagier game – very much in keeping with the usual League fare offered by

---

**FA CUP SEMI-FINAL
4 APRIL 1993**

Arsenal (0) 1
(Adams)

Tottenham Hotspur (0) 0
(White Hart Lane)

Arsenal:
Seaman - Dixon, Winterburn, Davis, Linighan, Adams, Jensen, Wright (O'Leary), Campbell, Merson, Parlour (Smith).

Tottenham Hotspur:
Thorstvedt - Austin, Edinburgh, Samways (Barmby), Mabbutt, Ruddock, Sedgley (Bergsson), Nayim, Anderton, Sheringham, Allen.

Captain's winner: Tony Adams scores the winning goal in the FA Cup Semi-Final in 1993

**FA PREMIER LEAGUE
11 MAY 1993**

Arsenal (0) 1
(Dickov)

Tottenham Hotspur (1)3
(Sheringham, Hendry 2)
(Highbury)

Arsenal:
Miller; Lydersen
(McGowan), Keown,
Marshall, O'Leary, Bould,
Flatts (Carter), Selley,
Smith, Dickov, Heaney.

Tottenham Hotspur:
Walker; McDonald, Van
Den Hauwe, Hill, Mabbutt,
Ruddock, Sedgley, Hendry
(Hodges), Anderton,
Sheringham, Allen.

the North London derby.

Vinny Samways had an early chance for Spurs after Adams miscued a backpass, but otherwise Ray Parlour and John Jensen did an effective job in front of the defence, restricting the opportunities Darren Anderton and Teddy Sheringham had to attack the Arsenal goal.

The winning goal was classic Arsenal: Paul Davis floated a free kick across the Tottenham penalty area and captain Tony Adams charged through to nod the ball powerfully past Erik Thorstvedt in the Spurs goal.

It was almost an exact replica of the goal Adams had scored in the quarter-final to beat Ipswich, and inspired the T-shirt slogan "Donkey won the derby!", sported proudly around Highbury over the following months.

The only blot on this successful bid to set the record straight was Lee Dixon's sending-off in the closing minutes, having embroiled himself in a petty tangle with Justin Edinburgh which earned him a second yellow card – and ruled him out of the Coca-Cola Cup final.

But the immediate target had been achieved: the old enemy had been put in their place in English foot-

ball's grandest setting, and history beckoned.

This result may have given Spurs their first League double over Arsenal in nearly 20 years, and nudged them ahead of the Gunners in the final League positions, but Arsenal obviously had their minds focussed on more important concerns.

With the Coca-Cola Cup already won and the FA Cup Final just five days away, George Graham took the opportunity to rest his key players and give someone else a chance, particularly young talents such as Paul Dickov, Mark Flatts and Scott Marshall.

Tottenham themselves had an unfamiliar look, giving rare first-team places to David McDonald, Lee Hodges and John Hendry. It was Hendry who made the most profitable use of his chance, scoring two goals by which to remember his fledgling Tottenham career.

A 3–1 victory was scant consolation to Spurs fans for the Cup semi-final defeat in April and (Hendry's booking for over-indulgent celebrations apart) there was little to suggest the drama poised to envelop both clubs just a few days later – for Arsenal, the FA Cup Final and replay; for Tottenham, Alan Sugar's sudden dismissal of Terry Venables from White Hart Lane.

1993–94

Arsenal had been given an unpleasant jolt in their first game of the new season, a Mick Quinn hat-trick giving Coventry a 3–0 opening-day win at Highbury. It was imperative, then, for the players to salvage some pride and credibility in their next game, and what better way to do so than beating Spurs at White Hart Lane?

To achieve that end, Graham controversially dropped both Limpar and Merson, fielding instead

**FA PREMIER LEAGUE
16 AUGUST 1993**

Tottenham Hotspur (0) 0

Arsenal (0)1
(Wright)
(White Hart Lane)

Tottenham Hotspur:
Thorstvedt; Austin,
Campbell, Samways,
Calderwood, Mabbutt,
Sedgley, Durie, Dozzell,
Sheringham, Howells
(Caskey).

Arsenal:
Seaman; Keown,
Winterburn, Davis,
Linighan, Adams, Jensen,
Wright, Campbell, Parlour,
McGoldrick.

the more pragmatic and reliable Ray Parlour and Eddie McGoldrick, but it was a tactic which succeeded in snuffing out the Tottenham threat, and ensured that Ian Wright's close-range header in the 87th minute snatched the points from under Spurs' noses.

Ray's away... Parlour escapes from Tottenham's Vinny Samways in a 1–0 win in 1993

**FA PREMIER LEAGUE
6 DECEMBER 1993**

Arsenal (0) 1
(Wright)
Tottenham Hotspur (1) 1
(Anderton)
(White Hart Lane)
Arsenal:
Seaman; Dixon, Keown,
Selley, Bould, Adams,
Jensen, Wright, Smith
(Campbell), Merson,
Limpar.
Tottenham Hotspur:
Thorstvedt; Kerslake,
Edinburgh, Samways
(Austin), Calderwood,
Sedgley, Caskey (Hendry),
Hazard, Anderton, Dozzell,
Campbell.

The scoreline could have been even more impressive had Kevin Campbell not spurned a hatful of chances, clearly showing that the confidence and composure he had displayed in previous seasons was sadly missing.

Arsenal went into the return game again on the back of a Quinn-inspired defeat at the hands of Coventry. This time, however, there were unable to defeat their North London rivals – a disappointment, considering that the Gunners were doing well at fourth in the table while Spurs were rapidly becoming immersed in a perilous relegation battle at the other end of the table.

Tottenham took the lead, however, with Darren Anderton scoring a deserved goal on 25 minutes, reflecting Tottenham's first-half dominance.

Arsenal were a changed side in the second half, however, and the inevitable equalizer came with 25 minutes left – Anders Limpar was the provider, Ian Wright the unfailing scorer, and Tottenham left Highbury lucky to hold on to a share of the points.

1994–95

Yet again the Sky TV cameras were focused on the North London derby, presumably more in expectation of an intriguing occasion than of an exciting spectacle.

This time it was Tottenham who entered the fixture with greater buoyancy, the arrival of Gerry Francis as manager in November having begun a rebuilding process which had made the Spurs defence much tighter than in recent years. Francis had never lost to Arsenal as a manager, and was obviously keen to end his first North London derby as a winner.

So too was Spurs' German striker Jürgen Klinsmann, making his first appearance in the famous fixture, and obviously the focus of attention for both the viewers and the Arsenal defence.

It was Tottenham's other big-name foreign import,

**FA PREMIER LEAGUE
JANUARY 1995**

Tottenham Hotspur (1) 1
(Popescu)
Arsenal (0) 0
(White Hart Lane)
Tottenham Hotspur:
Walker; Austin, Campbell,
Popescu (Nethercott),
Calderwood, Mabbutt,
Anderton, Howells,
Klinsmann, Sheringham,
Rosenthal.
Arsenal:
Seaman; Dixon,
Winterburn, Schwarz,
Bould, Linighan, Jensen,
Wright, Campbell, Selley
(Smith), Parlour.

however, who struck the winning goal, the Romanian midfielder Gica Popescu arriving in the Arsenal penalty area on 22 minutes to steer the ball securely past David Seaman.

Although the game was fairly evenly matched, Arsenal were always struggling to get back on level terms; and when Stefan Schwarz showed his frustration with a rash tackle on David Howells as the game neared the final whistle, referee Mike Reed had little option but to show the Swede the red card – a miserable end to a disappointing night for the Gunners.

The unsavoury element of the North London derbies came to the fore at Highbury. Bitterness between rival fans erupted, with bottles being thrown dangerously on to the field of play and numerous clashes both inside and outside the ground.

If the atmosphere of the fixture was typically tense, then the action on the field was also familiar from previous derby games. Arsenal broke the deadlock after an hour had been played when Justin Edinburgh gifted them a penalty, which Ian Wright gratefully despatched.

The lead lasted for just 13 minutes, however, before Klinsmann scored his first and last goal in a North London derby, securing a share of the spoils before the players swiftly left the pitch for the safety of the dressing rooms.

1995–96

Dennis Bergkamp could not have hoped for a more ideal introduction to the unique atmosphere of the North London derby: after just 14 minutes, the Dutchman sent a clinical strike flying past Ian Walker into the Tottenham goal.

A quarter of an hour later, however, Teddy Sheringham notched up an equalizer for the home side; and despite some surging runs from Paul

---

FA PREMIER LEAGUE
29 APRIL 1995

Arsenal (0) 1
    (Wright pen)
Tottenham Hotspur (0) 1
    (Klinsmann) (Highbury)

Arsenal:
    Seaman: Dixon, Winterburn, Schwarz, Bould, Adams, Keown, Wright, Hartson, Merson, Helder (Parlour).

Tottenham Hotspur:
    Thorstvedt; Kerslake, Edinburgh, Samways (Austin), Calderwood, Sedgley, Caskey (Hendry), Hazard, Anderton, Dozzell, Campbell.

Merson and some deft touches from Bergkamp, Spurs began to take advantage of the surprisingly open conditions of the game, and looked the more likely to score a winning goal.

That goal came nine minutes into the second half, when summer signing Chris Armstrong justified his £4.5 million price tag, controlling the ball neatly before striking it beyond David Seaman to wrap up the points.

For Armstrong, who supported Arsenal as a boy, and Bergkamp, who idolized Tottenham and Glenn Hoddle, it was a strange state of affairs: for Arsenal fans, it was a bitter setback after Bruce Rioch had made an encouraging start to the season.

The usual intensity of the derby games possessed an extra edge on this occasion, with the closing weeks of the season offering both clubs the possibility of UEFA Cup qualification. However, with both sides having fared disappointingly over the Easter period, the battle was likely to be fierce.

With Euro '96 firmly on the horizon, too, and the Sky cameras again relocating in North London, there was a lot at stake for the players on display.

The major boost for Tottenham was the appearance of Darren Anderton on the substitutes' bench, after a season ravaged by injury which had stopped him from playing in the first team since October.

Anderton made an appearance for the last 15 minutes of the game – time enough for him to get booked and to threaten to break clear of the Arsenal

---

FA PREMIER LEAGUE
18 NOVEMBER 1995

Tottenham Hotspur (1) 2
    (Sheringham, Armstrong)

Arsenal (1)1
    (Bergkamp)
    (White Hart Lane)

Tottenham Hotspur:
    Walker: Austin, Campbell, Howells, Calderwood, Mabbutt, Fox, Dozzell, Armstrong, Sheringham, Rosenthal (McMahon).

Arsenal:
    Seaman: Dixon, Winterburn, Keown, Bould, Adams, Platt, Hartson, Merson, Bergkamp, Helder (Hillier).

FA PREMIER LEAGUE
15 APRIL 1996

Arsenal (0) 0
Tottenham Hotspur (0) 0
    (Highbury)

Arsenal:
    Seaman: Dixon, Winterburn, Keown, Marshall, Linighan, Platt, Wright, Merson (Helder), Bergkamp, Parlour.

Tottenham Hotspur:
    Walker: Edinburgh, Wilson, Howells, Campbell (Nethercott), Mabbutt, Fox, Dozzell (Anderton), Armstrong, Sheringham, Rosenthal.

---

defence once, only to be thwarted by some sterling backtracking.

Anderton's arrival provided the main interest in a predictably cagey affair, Arsenal coping well despite the absence of both Tony Adams and Steve Bould, which forced Rioch to field a central defence comprising veteran Andy Linighan and youngster Scott Marshall.

The most intriguing battle was that between the irrepressible Ian Wright and Tottenham's commanding young centre-back Sol Campbell, who was running into the confident form which saw him win a place in England's Euro '96 squad alongside the likes of Adams, Sheringham and Anderton – although it would be Arsenal who grabbed the UEFA Cup place on the final day of the season.

1996–97

No. 2: Tony Adams blasts past Spurs in 1996

For too long, Arsenal fans had been haunted by the scoreline 3–1 – the two numbers which instantly conjured up memories of that FA Cup semi-final in 1991 and which acted as a potent weapon for crowing Spurs fans to brandish in the absence of any White Hart Lane-bound silverware.

Then, thanks to an astonishing last couple of minutes, Arsenal claimed their own famous 3–1 victory to remember – although with the drama all crammed in at the end rather than at the beginning.

Arsenal dominated the first half, finally gaining reward for their superiority when Spurs full-back Clive Wilson clumsily tangled with Dennis Bergkamp

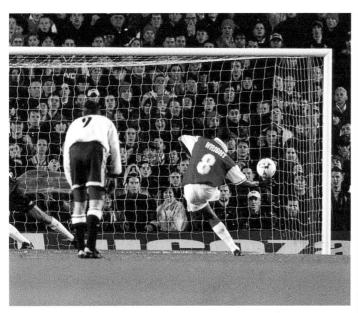

Hitting home. Ian Wright scores from a penalty for the first goal against Tottenham in 1996

in the Tottenham penalty area, finally tugging at the Arsenal striker and conceding a penalty. Ian Wright stepped up and struck the ball past Ian Walker to give the Gunners a half-time lead.

**FA PREMIER LEAGUE
24 NOVEMBER 1996**

Arsenal (1) 3
(Wright pen, Adams, Bergkamp)

Tottenham Hotspur (0) 1
(Sinton) (Highbury)

Arsenal:
Lukic: Dixon, Winterburn, Keown, Bould, Adams, Platt (Parlour), Wright, Merson, Bergkamp (Hartson), Vieira.

Tottenham Hotspur:
Walker: Carr, Wilson, Howells, Calderwood, Campbell, Sinton, Nielsen, Anderton, Sheringham, Armstrong

Lukic was standing in for the injured David Seaman, and it looked as though his moment of embarrassment would grant Tottenham a point: that is, until skipper Tony Adams made a typically gallant (but untypically flamboyant) contribution, with just two minutes left on the clock.

Spurs' equalizer came in controversial circumstances, after Arsenal had put the ball out of play for an injury on one of their players to be treated. Instead of returning the ball to the team that kicked it off, as custom and politeness dictate, the Tottenham players renewed their attack with renewed vigour after the throw-in and, taking the Arsenal defence by surprise, Andy Sinton darted a speculative shot which rebounded off the woodwork and bounced into the net off the unfortunate goalkeeper that day John Lukic.

The rain was pouring as Arsenal moved forward as one, led once more by Tony Adams.

Taking advantage of uncertainty in the Tottenham area, Adams flicked the ball up in the air in his stride before sending a crashing volley cannoning spectacularly billowing into the Tottenham net.

The surprise at such a glorious goal from the newly-adventurous Adams was matched only by rampant celebrations as Arsenal suddenly caught sight of victory in Wenger's first North London derby as manager at Highbury.

The thrills were not yet over, either, as there was still time for Wright, with a stunning display of ball control and passing accuracy, to jink past the struggling Wilson, look up and cross the ball for Bergkamp, who neatly turned inside Steve Carr before flicking the ball over Walker for an incredible third goal.

It was a fitting reward for Bergkamp, who had been the most inspirational player on the field throughout the match – although he could scarcely have imagined that the triumph would come in such dramatic, and glorious circumstances. Future Highbury derbies will do well to live up to that victory.

After the rapture of the Highbury game, it was perhaps inevitable that the return match would be less spellbinding.

Once again Arsenal were missing the injured David Seaman, but this time John Lukic could leave the field with greater satisfaction after making a succession of crucial saves to deny Steve Carr, Steffen Iversen and Darren Anderton as Spurs tried to exploit home advantage to salvage some pride from a sorry season.

However, the Arsenal defence was equal to the threats posed by the young Norwegian star, with Anderton and Sinton struggling to produce anything tangible from some attractive build-up play, the Gunners were apparently content to settle for the draw.

It all made for a frustrating afternoon for Ian Wright and Dennis Bergkamp, who rarely saw the ball in the Tottenham Hotspur half, let alone had a realistic chance of scoring.

**FA PREMIER LEAGUE
15 FEBRUARY 1997**

Tottenham Hotspur (0) 0

Arsenal (0)0
(White Hart Lane)

Tottenham Hotspur:
Walker: Austin, Edinburgh, Howells, Calderwood, Campbell, Carr, Rosenthal, Anderton, Iversen, Sinton.

Arsenal:
Lukic: Dixon, Winterburn, Keown, Bould, Adams, Parlour, Wright, Merson (Hughes), Bergkamp, Vieira.

Chapter 12
The Records

COCA-COLA CUP

Date	Team	Venue	Att	Score	Scorer
2nd Round					
1st L 22 Sept	Millwall	H	20,940	1–1	Campbell
2nd L 6 Oct	Millwall	A	18,500	1–1	Campbell
3rd Round					
28 October	Derby	A	22,208	1–1	Campbell
Dec 1	Derby	H	24,587	2–1	Wright, Campbell
4th Round					
6 Jan	Scarborough	A	6261	0–1	Winterburn
5th Round					
	Nottingham F	H	25,600	2–0	Wright 2
Semi-final					
10 Mar	Crystal Palace	H	28,584	2–0	Linighan, Wright
Final					
18 April	Sheffield W		74,007	2–1	Merson, Morrow

FA CUP

Date	Team	Venue	Att	Score	Scorer
3rd Round					
2 Jan	Yeovil	A	8,612	3–1	Wright 3
4th Round					
25 Jan	Leeds	H	24,516	2–2	Parlour, Merson
4th Round REPLAY					
25 Jan	Leeds	H	24,516	2–2	Parlour, Merson
5th Round					
13 Feb	Nottingham Forest	H	27,591	2–0	Wright 2
6th Round					
6 Mar	Ipswich	A	22,054	4–2	Adams, Wright (pen), Whelan (og), Campbell
Semi-final					
4 Apr	Tottenham	H	76.263	1–0	Adams
final at Wembley					
15 May	Sheffield W		79,347	1–1	Wright
final at Wembley					
20 May	Sheffield W		62,267	2–1	Wright, Linighan

Year-by-year statistics

Season 1992–93

PLAYER APPEARANCES					
Name	**App**	**(Sub)**	**Gls**	**Coca-Cola Cup Goals**	**FA Cup Goals**
Seaman	39				
Adams	33	2			
Campbell	32	5	4	4	1
Merson	32	1	6	1	1
Wright	30	1	15	5 (1 Pen)	10 (1 pen)
Dixon	29				
Jensen	29				
Winterburn	29		1	1	
Hillier	27	3	1		
Smith	27	4	3		1
Bould	24		1		
Linighan	19	2	2	1	1
Parlour	16		5	1	1
Keown	15	1			
Morrow	13	3		1	
Limpar	12	11	2		
Carter	11	5	2		
Selley	9				
Lyderson	7	1			
Davis	6				
O'Leary	6	5			
Flatts	6	4			
Miller	3	1			
Marshall	2				
Pates	2	5			
Dickov	1	2	2		
McGowan	–	2			
Groves	–	1			

Date	Team	Venue	Att	Score	Scorer
15 Aug	Norwich City	H	24,030	2–4	Bould, Campbell
18 Aug	Blackburn Rovers	A	16,434	0–1	
23 Aug	Liverpool	A	34,961	2–0	Limpar, Wright
26 Aug	Oldham Ath	H	20,796	2–0	Winterburn, Wright
29 Aug	Sheffield W	H	23,389	2–1	Parlour, Merson
2 Sept	QPR	A	20,868	0–0	
5 Sept	Wimbledon	A	12,906	2–3	Wright 2
12 Sept	Blackburn R	H	28,643	0–1	
19 Sept	Sheffield U	A	19,105	1–1	Wright
28 Sept	Manchester C	H	21,504	1–0	Wright
3 Oct	Chelsea	H	27,780	2–1	Merson, Wright
17 Oct	Nottingham F	A	24,862	1–0	Smith
24 Oct	Everton	H	28,052	2–0	Wright, Limpar
2 Nov	Crystal Palace	A	20,287	2–1	Merson, Wright
7 Nov	Coventry C	H	27,693	3–0	Smith, Wright, Campbell
21 Nov	Leeds U	A	30,516	0–3	
28 Nov	Manchester U	H	28,739	0–1	
5 Dec	Southampton	A	17,286	0–2	
12 Dec	Tottenham H	A	33,707	0–1	
19 Dec	Middlesbrough	H	23,197	1–1	Wright
26 Dec	Ipswich T	H	26,198	0–0	
28 Dec	Aston Villa	A	35,170	0–1	
9 Jan	Sheffield U	H	23,818	1–1	Hillier
16 Jan	Manchester C	A	25,051	1–0	Merson
31 Jan	Liverpool	H	27,580	0–1	
10 Feb	Wimbledon	H	18,253	0–1	
20 Feb	Oldham Ath	A	12,311	1–0	Linighan
24 Feb	Leeds U	H	21,061	0–1	
1 Mar	Chelsea	A	17,725	0–1	
3 Mar	Norwich	A	14,802	1–1	Wright
13 Mar	Coventry C	A	15,437	2–0	Campbell, Wright
20 Mar	Southampton	H	24,149	4–3	Linighan, Merson, Carter 2
24 Mar	Manchester U	A	37,301	0–0	
6 Apr	Middlesbrough	A	12,726	0–1	
10 Apr	Ipswich T	A	20,358	2–1	Smith, Merson
12 Apr	Aston Villa	H	27,123	0–1	
21 Apr	Nottingham F	H	19,044	1–1	Wright
1 May	Everton	A	19,044	0–0	
4 May	QPR	H	18.817	0–0	
6 May	Sheffield W	A	23,645	0–1	
8 May	Crystal Palace	H	25,225	3–0	Wright, Dickov, Campbell
11 May	Tottenham H	H	26,393	1–3	Dickov

Final League Position : 10

Season 1993–94

COCA-COLA CUP

Date	Team	Venue	Att	Score	Scorer
2nd Round					
1st L 21 Sept	Huddersfield T	A	14,275	5–0	Wright 3, Campbell, Merson
2nd L 5 Oct	Huddersfield T	H	18,789	1–1	Smith
3rd Round					
1st L 26 Oct	Norwich C	H	24,539	1–1	Wright
2nd L 9 Nov	Norwich C	A	16,319	3–0	Wright 2, Merson
4th Round					
30 Nov	Aston Villa	H	26,453	0–1	Atkinson

FA CUP

Date	Team	Venue	Att	Score	Scorer
3rd Round					
9 Jan	Millwall	A	20,093	1–0	
4th Round					
31 Jan	Bolton	A	18,891	2–2	Wright, Adams
4th Round REPLAY					
9 Feb	Bolton W	H	33,863	1–3	McGinlay, McAteer, Walker

PLAYER RECORDS

Name	App	(Sub)	L. Goals	Other Goals
Seaman	39			
Wright	39		23 (5 pens)	6 Coca-Cola Cup, 1 FA Cup
Adams	35			2 FA Cup
Winterburn	34			
Dixon	32	1		
Campbell	28	9	14	1 Coca-Cola Cup
Jensen	27			
Merson	24	9	7	
Parlour	24	3	2	
Keown	23	10		
Bould	23	2	1	3 OG
McGoldrick	23	3		
Smith	21	4	3	1 Coca-Cola Cup, 1 FA Cup goal
Davis	21	1		
Linighan	20	1		
Selley	16	2		
Hillier	11	4		
Limpar	9	1		
Morrow	7	4		
Miller	3	1		
Flatts	2	1		
Heaney	1			
Dickov	–	1		

Celebration: Kevin Campbell and friends during the 1993 game against Swindon that Arsenal won 4–0

	FA PREMIER LEAGUE				
Date	**Team**	**Venue**	**Att**	**Score**	**Scorer**
14 Aug	Coventry C	H	26,397	0–3	
16 Aug	Tottenham H	A	28,355	1–0	Wright
21 Aug	Sheffield W	A	26,023	1–0	Wright
24 Aug	Leeds U	H	29,042	2–1	Newsome (og) Merson
28 Aug	Everton	H	29,063	2–0	Wright 2
1 Sept	Blackburn R	A	14,410	1–1	Campbell
11 Sept	Ipswich T	H	28,563	4–0	Wright, Campbell 3
19 Sept	Manchester U	A	44,009	0–1	
25 Sept	Southampton	H	26,902	1–0	Merson
2 Oct	Liverpool	A	29,567	0–0	
16 Oct	Manchester C	H	29,567	0–0	
23 Oct	Oldham Ath	A	12,105	0–0	
30 Oct	Norwich C	H	30,516	0–0	
6 Nov	Aston Villa	H	31,773	1–2	Wright
20 Nov	Chelsea	A	26,839	2–0	Smith, Wright (pen)
24 Nov	West Ham U	A	20,279	0–0	
27 Nov	Newcastle U	H	36,091	2–1	Wright, Smith
4 Dec	Coventry C	A	12,632	0–1	
6 Dec	Tottenham H	H	35,669	1–1	Wright
12 Dec	Sheffield W	H	22,026	1–0	Wright
18 Dec	Leeds U	A	37,289	1–2	Campbell
27 Dec	Swindon T	A	17,212	4–0	Campbell 3, Wright
29 Dec	Sheffield U	H	27,035	3–0	Campbell 2, Wright
1 Jan	Wimbledon	A	16,584	3–0	Campbell, Parlour, Wright
3 Jan	QPR	H	34,935	0–0	
15 Jan	Manchester C	A	26, 524	0–0	
22 Jan	Oldham Ath	H	26,524	1–1	Wright (pen)
13 Feb	Norwich C	A	17,667	1–1	Campbell
19 Feb	Everton	A	19,760	1–1	Merson
25 Feb	Blackburn R	H	35,030	0–0	
5 Mar	Ipswich T	A	18, 803	5–1	Wright 3 (1 pen), Youds (og) , Parlour
19 Mar	Southampton	A	16,790	4–0	Wright 3 (1 pen), Campbell
22 Mar	Manchester U	H	36,023	2–2	Pallister (og), Merson
26 Mar	Liverpool	H	31,634	1–0	Merson
2 Apr	Swindon T	H	31,635	1–1	Smith
4 Apr	Sheffield U	A	20,019	1–1	Campbell
16 Apr	Chelsea	H	34,314	1–0	Wright
19 Apr	Wimbledon	H	21,292	1–1	Bould
23 Apr	Aston Villa	A	31,580	2–1	Wright 2 (1 pen)
27 Apr	QPR	A	11,442	1–1	Merson
30 Apr	West Ham U	H	33,700	0–2	
7 May	Newcastle U	A	32,216	0–2	

Final League Position: 4

Season 1994–95

FA PREMIER LEAGUE					
Date	**Team**	**Venue**	**Att**	**Score**	**Scorer**
20 Aug	Manchester C	H	38,368	3–0	Campbell, Coton (og), Wright
23 Aug	Leeds U	A	34,318	0–1	
28 Aug	Liverpool	A	30,017	0–3	
31 Aug	Blackburn R	H	37,629	0–0	
10 Sept	Norwich C	A	17,768	0–0	
18 Sept	Newcastle U	H	36,819	2–3	Adams, Wright
25 Sept	West Ham U	A	18,495	2–0	Adams, Wright
1 Oct	Crystal Palace	H	34,316	1–2	Wright
8 Oct	Wimbledon	A	10,842	3–1	Wright, Smith, Campbell
15 Oct	Chelsea	H	38,234	3–1	Wright 2, Campbell
23 Oct	Coventry C	H	31,725	2–1	Wright 2
29 Oct	Everton	A	32,005	1–1	Schwarz
6 Nov	Sheffield W	H	33,705	0–0	
19 Nov	Southampton	A	15,201	0–1	
23 Nov	Leicester C	A	20,774	1–2	Wright (pen)
26 Nov	Manchester U	H	38,301	0–0	
3 Dec	Nottingham F	A	21,662	2–2	Keown, Davis
12 Dec	Manchester C	A	20,500	2–1	Smith, Schwarz
17 Dec	Leeds U	H	38,100	1–3	Linighan
26 Dec	Aston Villa	H	34,452	0–0	
28 Dec	Ipswich T	A	22,047	2–0	Wright, Campbell
31 Dec	QPR	H	32,393	1–3	Jensen
2 Jan	Tottenham H	A	28,747	0–1	
14 Jan	Everton	H	34,743	1–1	Wright
21 Jan	Coventry C	A	14,557	1–0	Hartson
24 Jan	Southampton	H	27,213	1–1	Hartson
4 Feb	Sheffield W	A	23,468	1–3	Linighan
11 Feb	Leicester C	H	31,373	1–1	Merson
21 Feb	Nottingham F	H	35,441	1–0	Kiwomya
25 Feb	Crystal Palace	A	17,063	3–0	Merson, Kiwomya 2
5 Mar	West Ham U	H	36,295	0–1	
8 Mar	Blackburn R	A	23,452	1–3	Morrow
19 Mar	Newcastle U	A	35,611	0–1	
22 Mar	Manchester U	A	43,623	0–3	
1 Apr	Norwich C	H	36,942	5–1	Hartson 2, Dixon, Merson, Newman (og)
8 Apr	QPR	A	16,341	1–3	Adams
12 Apr	Liverpool	H	38,036	0–1	
15 Apr	Ipswich T	H	36,818	4–1	Merson, Wright 3
17 Apr	Aston Villa	A	32,005	4–0	Hartson 2, Wright 2 (1 pen)
29 Apr	Tottenham H	H	38,377	1–1	Wright (pen)
4 May	Wimbledon	H	32,822	0–0	
14 May	Chelsea	A	29,542	1–2	Hartson

Final League Position: 12

FA CUP

Date	Team	Venue	Att	Score	Scorer
3rd Round					
Jan 7	Millwall	H	17,715	0–0	

PLAYER RECORDS

Name	App	(Sub)	L. Goals	Other Goals
Seaman	39			
Dixon	39			
Seaman	31			
Winterburn	39			
Schwarz	34			
Bould	30	1		
Wright	30	1	18 (3 pens)	3 Coca-Cola Cup
Adams	27		3	1 Coca-Cola Cup
Keown	24	7		
Merson	24		4	1 Coca-Cola Cup
Jensen	24		1	
Parlour	22	8		
Campbell	19	4	4	1 Coca-Cola Cup
Smith	17	2	2	1 Coca-Cola Cup
Hartson	14	1	7	
Linighan	13	7	2	
Helder	12	1		
Morrow	11	4	1	2 OG
Bartram	11			
Selley	10	3		
McGoldrick	9	2		
Kiwomya	5	9	3	
Hillier	5	4		
Dickov	4	5		
Davis	3	1	1	
Carter	2	1		
Flatts	1	2		
Hughes	1			
McGowan	1			
Clarke	–	1		
Shaw	–	1		

COCA-COLA CUP

Date	Team	Venue	Att	Score	Scorer
2nd Round					
1st L 21 Sept	Hartlepool	A	4,421	5–0	Adams, Smith, Wright 2, Merson
5 Oct	Hartlepool	H	20,520	2–0	Campbell, Dickov
3rd Round					
1st L 26 Oct	Oldham Ath	A	9,303	0–0	
3rd Round Replay					
9 Nov	Oldham Ath	H	22,746		Dickov 2
4th Round					
30 Nov	Sheffield	W	27,390	2–0	Morrow, Wright
5th Round					
11 Jan	Liverpool	A	35,026	0–1	

He's off! Ray Parlour dances the ball around the QPR defence in the Premiership match on 31 December 1994. Arsenal lost 3–1

Season 1995–96

	FA PREMIER LEAGUE				
Date	Team	Venue	Att	Score	Scorer
20 Aug	Middlesbrough	H	37,308	1–1	Wright
23 Aug	Everton	A	36,047	2–0	Platt, Wright
26 Aug	Coventry C	A	20,081	0–0	
29 Aug	Nottingham F	H	38,248	1–	Platt
10 Sept	Manchester C	A	23,984	1–0	Wright
16 Sept	West Ham U	H	38,065	1–0	Wright (pen)
23 Sept	Southampton	H	38,136	4–2	Bergkamp 2, Adams , Wright
30 Sept	Chelsea	A	31,048	0–1	
14 Oct	Leeds U	A	38,332	3–0	Merson, Bergkamp, Wright
21 Oct	Aston Villa	H	38,271	2–0	Merson, Wright
30 Oct	Bolton W	A	18,682	0–1	
4 Nov	Manchester U	H	38,317	1–0	Bergkamp
18 Nov	Tottenham H	A	32,894	1–2	Bergkamp
21 Nov	Sheffield W	H	34,556	4–2	Bergkamp, Winterburn, Dickov, Hartson
26 Nov	Blackburn R	H	37,695	0–0	
2 Dec	Aston Villa	A	37,770	1–1	Platt
9 Dec	Southampton	A	15,238	0–0	
16 Dec	Chelsea	H	38,295	1–1	Dixon
23 Dec	Liverpool	A	39,806	1–3	Wright (pen)
26 Dec	QPR	H	38,259	3–0	Wright, Merson 2
30 Dec	Wimbledon	H	37,640	1–3	Wright
2 Jan	Newcastle U	A	36,530	0–2	
13 Jan	Middlesbrough	A	29,539	3–2	Merson, Platt, Helder
20 Jan	Everton	H	38,275	1–2	Wright
3 Feb	Coventry C	H	35, 623	1–1	Bergkamp
10 Feb	Nottingham F	A	27,222	1–0	Bergkamp
24 Feb	West Ham U	A	24,217	1–0	Hartson
2 Mar	QPR	A	17,970	1–1	Bergkamp
5 Mar	Manchester C	H	34,519	3–1	Hartson 2, Dixon
16 Mar	Wimbledon	A	18,335	3–0	Winterburn, Platt, Bergkamp
20 Mar	Manchester U	A	50,028	0–1	
23 Mar	Newcastle U	H	38,271	2–0	Marshall, Wright
6 Apr	Leeds U	H	37,619	2–1	Wright 2
8 Apr	Sheffield W	A	24,349	0–1	
15 Apr	Tottenham H	H	38,273	0–0	
27 Apr	Blackburn R	A	29,834	1–1	Wright (pen)
1 May	Liverpool	H	38,323	0–0	
5 May	Bolton W	H	38,104	2–1	Platt, Bergkamp

Final League Position: 5

FA CUP

Date	Team	Venue	Att	Score	Scorer
3rd Round					
6 Jan	Sheffield U	H	33,453	1–1	Wright
3rd Round Replay					
17 Jan	Sheffield U	A	22,255	0–1	

PLAYER RECORDS

Name	App	(Sub)	L. Goals	Other Goals
Seaman	38			
Dixon	38			
Merson	38			
Winterburn	36			
Keown	34		1	
Bergkamp	33		11	5 Coca-Cola Cup
Wright	31		15 (3 pens)	7 Coca-Cola Cup (1 pen), 1 FA Cup
Platt	27	2	6	
Adams	21		1	2 Coca-Cola Cup
Parlour	20	2		
Bould	19			1 Coca-Cola Cup
Linighan	17	1		
Helder	15	9	1	
Hartson	15	4	4	1 Coca-Cola Cup
Jensen	13	2		
Marshall	10	1	1	
Clarke	4	2		
Hillier	3	2		
Morrow	3	1		
Rose	1	3		
Dickov	1	6	1	
McGowan	1			
Shaw	–	3		
McGoldrick	–	1		
Hughes	–	1		

COCA-COLA CUP

Date	Team	Venue	Att	Score	Scorer
2nd Round					
1st L 19 Sept	Hartlepool	A	4,945	3–0	Adams 2, Wright
2nd L 3 Oct	Hartlepool	H	27,194	5–0	Bergkamp 2, Wright 3
3rd Round					
24 Oct	Barnsley	A	18,429	3–0	Bould, Bergkamp, Keown
4th Round					
28 Nov	Sheffield W	H	35,361	2–1	Wright (pen), Hartson
5th Round					
10 Jan	Newcastle U	H	37,857	2–0	Wright 2
Semi-Final (Aston Villa won away on goals)					
1st L 14 Feb	Aston Villa	H	37,562	2–2	Bergkamp 2
2nd L 21 Feb	Aston Villa	A	39,334	0–0	

Ever-present... since joining, Nigel Winterburn has always been a regular on the team. This game, against his former club Chelsea, was won 1–0

Season 1996–97

Date	Team	Venue	Att	Score	Scorer
17 Aug	West Ham U	H	38,056	2–0	Bergkamp, Hartson
19 Aug	Liverpool	A	38,103	0–2	
24 Aug	Leicester C	A	20,429	2–0	Bergkamp, Wright
4 Sept	Chelsea	H	38,132	3–3	Keown, Merson, Wright
7 Sept	Aston Villa	A	37,944	2–2	Linighan, Merson
16 Sept	Sheffield W	H	33.461	4–1	Platt, Wright 3
21 Sept	Middlesbrough	A	29,629	2–0	Wright, Merson
28 Sep	Sunderland	H	38,016	2–0	Hartson, Parlour
12 Oct	Blackburn R	A	24,303	2–0	Wright 2
19 Oct	Coventry C	H	38,140	0–0	
26 Oct	Leeds U	H	38,076	3–0	Wright, Bergkamp, Dixon
2 Nov	Wimbledon	A	25,521	2–2	Wright, Merson
16 Nov	Manchester U	A	55,210	0–1	
24 Nov	Tottenham H	H	38,264	3–1	Adams, Wright, Bergkamp
30 Nov	Newcastle	A	36,565	2–1	Dixon, Wright
4 Dec	Southampton	H	38,033	3–1	Wright, Merson, Shaw
7 Dec	Derby C	H	38,018	2–2	Adams, Veira
21 Dec	Nottingham F	A	27,384	1–2	Wright
26 Dec	Sheffield W	A	23,245	0–0	
28 Dec	Aston Villa	H	38,130	2–2	Wright, Merson
1 Jan	Middlesbrough	H	37,573	2–0	Wright, Bergkamp
11 Jan	Sunderland	A	21,154	0–1	
19 Jan	Everton	H	38,095	3–1	Merson, Bergkamp
29 Jan	West Ham U	A	24,382	2–1	Parlour, Wright
1 Feb	Leeds U	A	35,502	0–0	
15 Feb	Tottenham H	A	33,309	0–0	
19 Feb	Manchester U	H	38,172	1–2	Bergkamp
23 Feb	Wimbledon	H	37,854	0–1	
1 Mar	Everton	A	36,980	2–0	Wright, Bergkamp
8 Mar	Nottingham F	H	38,206	2–0	Bergkamp 2
15 Mar	Southampton	A	15,144	2–0	Shaw, Hughes
24 Mar	Liverpool	H	38,068	1–2	Wright
5 Apr	Chelsea	A	28,182	3–0	Platt, Wright, Bergkamp
12 Apr	Leicester C	H	38,044	2–0	Adam, Platt
19 Apr	Blackburn R	H	38,086	1–1	Platt
21 Apr	Coventry C	A	19,998	1–1	Wright
3 May	Newcastle U	H	38,179	0–1	
11 May	Derby C	A	18,287	3–1	Wright 2, Bergkamp

Final League Position: 3

FA CUP

Date	Team	Venue	Att	Score	Scorer
3rd Round					
4 Jan	Sunderland	H	37,793	1–1	Hartson
3rd Round Replay					
15 Jan	Sunderland	A	15,277	2–0	Hughes, Bergkamp
4 Feb	Leeds U	H	38,115	0–1	

COCA-COLA CUP

Date	Team	Venue	Att	Score	Scorer
3rd Round					
23 Oct	Stoke C	A	20,804	1–1	Wright
3rd Round					
13 Nov	Stoke C	H	33,962	5–2	Platt, Wright 2, Bergkamp, Merson
4th Round					
27 Nov	Liverpool	A	32,814	2–4	Wright 2

PLAYER RECORDS

Name	App	(Sub)	L. Goals	Other Goals
Winterburn	38			
Bould	33			
Keown	33		1	
Merson	32		6	1 Coca-Cola Cup
Dixon	31	1	2	
Wright	30	5	23 (4 pens)	5 Coca-Cola Cup (3 pens)
Vieira	30	1	2	
Bergkamp	28	1	12 (3 pen)	1 Coca-Cola Cup 1 FA Cup goal
Adams	27	1	3	
Platt	27	1	4	1 Coca-Cola Cup 1 FA Cup goal
Seaman	22			
Parlour	17	13	2	
Lukic	15			
Hartson	14	5	3	1 FA Cup goal
Linighan	9	5	1	
Hughes	9	5	1	1 FA Cup goal
Garde	7	4		
Marshall	6	2		
Morrow	5	9		
Shaw	1	7	2	
McGowan	1			
Rose	1			
Harper	1			
Anelka	–	4		
Helder	–	2		
Dickov	–	1		
Selley	–	1		

Hat-trick: Ian Wright celebrates his third against Sheffield Wednesday

Miscellaneous Premiership records

Arsenal FC have, in their time, broken many records. Here we feature their records from the first five years of the Premier League.

Team Records

OVERALL RECORD						
P	W	D	L	F	A	Pts
202	82	63	57	256	183	309

Win ratio of 41%
Defeat ratio of 28%
Strike-rate ratio of 1.27 goals per game

HOME RECORD						
P	W	D	L	F	A	Pts
101	46	31	24	143	90	169

Win ratio of 46%
Defeat ratio of 24%
Strike-rate ratio of 1.42 goals per game

AWAY RECORD						
P	W	D	L	F	A	Pts
101	36	32	33	123	91	140

Win ratio of 36%
Defeat ratio of 32%
Strike-rate ratio of 1.22 goals per game

HIGHS AND LOWS

Biggest victories

5–1 vs. Ipswich Town (H) 1993–94
5–1 vs. Norwich City (H) 1994–95

Heaviest defeats

3–0 vs. Leeds United 1992–93
3–0 vs. Liverpool 1994–95

Biggest away victory

4–0 vs. Swindon T 1993–94, 5–1 vs. Ipswich T 1993–94,
4–0 vs. Southampton 1993–94, 4–0 vs. Aston Villa 1994–95

Heaviest home defeat

0–3 vs. Coventry C 1993–94

Most points

68 in season 1996–97 (position 3rd)

Fewest points

51 in season 1994–95 (position 12th)

Most goals for

62 in season 1996–97

Fewest goals for

40 in season 1992–93

Most goals against

49 in season 1994–95

Fewest goals against

28 in season 1993–94

Most victories

19 in season 1996–97

Fewest wins

13 in season 1994–95

Fewest defeats

7 in season 1993–94

Most defeats

17 in season 1994–95

Most draws

17 in season 1993–94

SEQUENCES AND TOTALS

Unbeaten sequence at home

12 games in season 1993–94 and 1996–97

Most home wins in a season

10 games in season 1993–94, 1995–96 and 1996–97

Longest run without a home win in a season

8 games in season 1994–95

Most home defeats in a season

7 games in season 1992–93

Most away wins in a season

9 games in season 1996–97

Most away defeats in a season

11 games in season 1994–95

Longest unbeaten run

10 games from 24 August 1996 to 16 November 1996

Longest run without a victory

8 games in season 1992–93

Worst run of results

One win between 21 November 1992 and 2 February 1993 (11 matches)

Most victories in a row

6 games in season 1992–93

Most home victories in a row

5 games in season 1995–96

Most away victories in a row

3 games in season 1996–97

Most defeats in a row

4 games in season 1992–93 and 1994–95

ATTENDANCES

Highest home attendance

38,377 vs. Tottenham Hotspur in season 1994–95

Highest away attendance

55,210 vs. Manchester United in season 1996–97

Individual Records

GOALSCORING

Best scoring in a season

23 goals by Ian Wright in seasons 1993–94 and 1996–97

Highest scorer (Premier League only)

Ian Wright 93 goals (1992 to 1997)

Top scorers per season

14 goals by Ian Wright in season 1992–93
23 goals by Ian Wright in season 1993–94
18 goals by Ian Wright in season 1994–95
15 goals by Ian Wright in season 1995–96
23 goals by Ian Wright in season 1996–97

Top five aggregate goalscorers (all-time)

1 Cliff Bastin 150 goals
2 Jimmy Brain 125 goals
3 Doug Lishman 125 goals
4 Ted Drake 124 goals
5 Ian Wright 118 goals

Most hat-tricks

4 by Ian Wright

APPEARANCES

Longest run of appearances

82 consecutive appearances by Paul Merson between 4 February 1995 and 1 March 1997

Top five aggregate appearances (all-time)

1 David O'Leary 558 appearances
2 George Armstrong 500 appearances
3 Bob John 421 appearances
4 Tony Adams 395 appearances
5 Eddie Hapgood 393 appearances

(Far left) Glory Boys... David Seaman and friend celebrating the crowning of Arsenal as the cup kings in 1993

Index

Acknowledgements

The publishers would like to thank the following sources for their kind permission to reproduce the pictures in this book:

Allsport UK Ltd./Shaun Botterill, Clive Brunskill, David Cannon, Graham Chadwick, Stu Forster, Ross Kinnaird, Alex Livesey, Gary Prior, Ben Radford, Mark Thompson; Allsport Historical Collection/Hulton Getty; Colorsport; Hulton Getty; M.S.I.; Popperfoto/Reuters

Every effort has been made to acknowledge correctly and contact the source and/copyright holder of each picture, and Carlton Books Limited apologises for any unintentional errors or omissions which will be corrected in future editions of this book.